Locking Shields

Real Men Pursuing a Real God

George Oakes

RIVER BIRCH PRESS

Daphne, Alabama

ISBN 978-1-951561-71-0 (print)
ISBN 978-1-951561-72-7 (e-book)

For Worldwide Distribution
Printed in the U.S.A.

River Birch Press
P.O. Box 868, Daphne, AL 36526

Contents

Acknowledgments

Lord Jesus, it never ceases to amaze me that You know me best and love me most, even when I'm not loveable. There are no words that could ever articulate how much You mean to me and how grateful I am to You. Thank you so much for all that You've done, and continue to do, in my life. May my light burn brightly for You. I love you too!

Tina, you are my biggest advocate. Unfortunately, you also have the unenviable role of being the one who has to speak truth to me regardless of the circumstance. You always do so from a place of love, wanting His best for me. For this, I am eternally grateful. I cannot imagine my life without you in it. I love you truly, madly, deeply.

To the guys who know me better than I'm comfortable with, who have spoken into my life, encouraged me, and pointed me to the cross—THANK YOU! Without your love, and the occasional kick in the pants, I would not be where I am. Know that you make a difference.

To Keith Carroll and Brian Banashak, I'm so grateful that you saw something of value in that first draft. Thank you for your expertise and for sharing your insights with me! May God continue to bless, lead, and guide you as you mentor and help others move forward with what He has placed in their hearts.

Preface

I had spent most of my life becoming someone I was never supposed to be when God gave me a clear warning that I needed to stop what I was doing. It rattled me, but I chose to ignore it. Living out the consequences of that choice was brutal. There were spiritual ramifications to whom I'd become that were suddenly very apparent, and there was a genuine battle for my future. I'd dug a deep hole and desperately wanted to be free but didn't know how to be different. All I knew was that I didn't want to be this version of "me" ever again. I was as low in life as I never wanted to be and needed God's help, not just to make it through, but to actually change, to be different. My only hope was the outstretched hand Jesus was offering. I grabbed it.

My early days of being a Christian were marked by trying to be different, devoting time to read the Bible and pray. I recognized that I was pretty limited in my ability to really understand what I was reading, much less move forward on my own. I didn't quite understand it at first, but what was needed was for someone to come alongside of me. I was accustomed to working out and understood that whether hitting the gym or running, having a partner to push and encourage you was a powerful thing. I was always able to do a couple more reps, add more weight, run a bit faster or go farther when I had a buddy, but I didn't know how to find one with what I was going through. I didn't have anyone that I could ask to step into that role.

God opened a door for me to join a men's group that met on Saturday mornings, and it was very much an answer to my prayer. I'll never forget the very first meeting I went to. I didn't know the guy who was hosting the group, but I got there a few minutes early and, taking a deep breath, knocked on the door. He quickly answered and greeted me with a giant, warm smile. He invited me in and immediately wrapped me in a manly embrace and prayed over me. Right there, just (and I mean "just" as in 18") inside the front door! To be honest, that still brings tears to my eyes. Mike became my battle buddy.

It was kinda weird at times, though. Something negative would start stirring up within me, and all of a sudden, my phone would ring. I'd answer in a less than victorious tone, and there would be Mike with a happy, "Hey! How ya doin' brother? Just felt I needed to check on ya. How's it goin'?" It still amazes me how God provides exactly what's needed at the precise moment it's needed.

Since then, I've been part of a men's group in one form or another as I've come to realize my ongoing need to be in a tight community of godly men. I've met a lot of guys that genuinely want to be in a men's group. They were either part of one in the past and it really impacted them, or they recognize a longing within and God is leading them in that direction. I've also met guys that say they want to be in a men's group but never actually take the steps to join one. The truth is that there are thousands of excuses to avoid signing up or showing up. The only reason we do is to engage with other men who are also pursing their relationship with Jesus Christ.

To be honest, men's groups are full of guys just like you and I. I've seen brawny, manly men, break down in tears as they talk about their shortcomings and what God is doing in their life. I've shed my fair share of tears as well and have learned not to feel ashamed for it. I can't tell you how many times I've heard someone say, "Man! I thought it was just me! I thought I was the only one dealing with this!" Nope. That's a lie designed to keep you isolated and your mouth shut.

We all have to draw a line in the sand at some point and say, "No more!" but few of us recognize that the drawing of that line has taken ground in Jesus' name. Every man in the group has stuff they're struggling with. Every man has hard-won victories that God has led them into. We get together and share what God is doing in our lives, what we're dealing with, and what we've been through. We meet on purpose and for a purpose. That purpose is the work of Jesus Christ being made manifest in our lives. By the way, nobody in the group has it all figured out, which is why we're there. We're all pursuing Jesus Christ and haven't "arrived" yet.

At its core, *Locking Shields* is a collection of lessons from a men's group. God used those meetings to bring about change in the lives of those who wanted it. The relationships formed there persist even though job changes and cross country moves have physically separated us. I need my brothers in Christ. I need that battle buddy who knows me better than I'm actually comfortable with. That battle buddy loves, encourages, challenges, and pushes me to be all that God designed, created, and purposed me to be. Nothing less will do. As it should be.

I know I'm not alone. This is something guys want and need whether we admit it or not. *Locking Shields* presents an opportunity to lock shields of faith with other men and advance the Kingdom of God. The intent of this collection of lessons is to provide a running start of sorts for those who want to lead, or simply be in, a men's group. My prayer is that this book will enable you to get started in that endeavor.

→1←

Why We Meet

If I had to provide a description for this group, I'd say that "We're brothers in Christ who band together to seek His face, to pursue who He says we are, and to move from where we are to where He wants us to be." The scripture references behind that are:

Let us not neglect our church meetings, as some people do, but encourage and warn each other, especially now that the day of his coming back again is drawing near (Hebrews 10:25, TLB).

As iron sharpens iron, so one person sharpens another (Proverbs 27:17, NIV).

If my people, who are called by my name, will humble themselves and pray and seek my face and turn from their wicked ways, then I will hear from heaven, and I will forgive their sin and will heal their land (2 Chronicles 7:14, NIV).

You should have as little desire for this world as a dead person does. Your real life is in heaven with Christ and God (Colossians 3:3, TLB).

There are three main reasons we meet:

1. We're here to pursue Jesus Christ and deepen our relationship with Him.

2. We're here to lock "Shields of Faith" with another Christian brother and drive the enemy of our soul back, taking new ground for our families.

3. We're here to encourage each other into greater obedience to God's Word.

Christian men are no different than those who eschew church in that we're still men, and we're still not perfect. Unfortunately, we seem to accept the lie that because we've asked Jesus into our heart that we suddenly have it covered. We've been forgiven for all that we've done, but frequently the repercussions from our struggle with pornography, substance abuse, anger, selfishness, etc. still have to be walked out. While we no longer seek to please only ourselves, but instead desire to please His heart, we still have many things to un-learn.

We're not alone in whatever it is we're dealing with. Chances are pretty high that someone in the room is dealing with, or has walked through, the same thing we are. Nobody has it all figured out. We all have things we fight against in our Christian walk. We all have things we're addicted to.

According to Dictionary.com, to be addicted means that there's something that we are "devoted (to) or given up to a practice or habit or to something psychologically or physiologically habit-forming." So, if there's something in our lives that we know shouldn't be there, but we keep going back to it—we're addicted to whatever that is. There has to be some sort of payoff in it for us, or we wouldn't keep going back and feeding it right?

One of the things I've struggled with since I was a kid is anger. Yes, anger was demonstrated at home, but I clearly remember feeling a surge of emotion and strength whenever I gave into it. I thought I was in control of it and had learned how to use it, but that was a lie. The truth is that anger controlled me. Not that I cared really. I didn't have a problem with my anger. My wife, however, had a problem with it, but I was pretty much okay with my anger.

I didn't keep reaching for anger simply out of habit or learned behavior; I reached for it because I liked certain parts of how it made me feel. I was addicted to the rush of emotion, the way I felt incredibly strong, and so on. The truth is that being angry was never supposed to be part of who I am. In order to have true change in my life, I needed God to show me the person He designed, created, and purposed me to be so that I could reframe the picture I have of myself. I want to take down who I made myself into and take on who God says I am.

Now, there are a couple things we don't do in here.

We don't talk about what other guys say. It's fine to share what the main discussion or topic was. Sharing what YOU said is fine, but don't go telling another man's story.

We don't psychoanalyze. Dr. Phil is not in the house. We offer God-given insight from our own spiritual journey. We talk about things God has shown us and is doing in us and give biblical advice and truth in love.

We don't do behavior modification. Behavior modification is me trying to do things differently and trying to move forward in my strength. Been there, done that, failed miserably. We're here to identify the heart issue behind what's going on and ask God to heal that area of our life and purify us. We ask God for opportunities to show His love to our families, to serve them, and to love them as they need to be loved instead of having to make do with what we have to offer on our own.

Discussion Questions

1. Why did you choose to come here?

2. What do you want to get out of this?

3. What part of "you" are you willing to give up in order to have more of Jesus Christ in your life?

→2←

What Do You Want Me to Do for You?

Solomon called together all the leaders of Israel—the generals and captains of the army, the judges, and all the political and clan leaders. Then he led the entire assembly to the place of worship in Gibeon, for God's Tabernacle was located there. (This was the Tabernacle that Moses, the Lord's servant, had made in the wilderness.) David had already moved the Ark of God from Kiriath-jearim to the tent he had prepared for it in Jerusalem. But the bronze altar made by Bezalel son of Uri and grandson of Hur was there at Gibeon in front of the Tabernacle of the Lord. So Solomon and the people gathered in front of it to consult the Lord. There in front of the Tabernacle, Solomon went up to the bronze altar in the Lord's presence and sacrificed 1,000 burnt offerings on it. That night God appeared to Solomon and said, "What do you want? Ask, and I will give it to you!" (2 Chronicles 1:2-7, NLT)

As Jesus and his disciples left town (Jericho), a large crowd followed him. A blind beggar named Bartimaeus (son of Timaeus) was sitting beside the road. When Bartimaeus heard that Jesus of Nazareth was nearby, he began to shout, "Jesus, Son of David, have mercy on me!" "Be quiet!" many of the people yelled at him. But he only shouted louder, "Son of David, have mercy on me!" When Jesus heard him, he stopped and said, "Tell him to come here." So they called the blind man. "Cheer up," they said. "Come on, he's calling you!" Bartimaeus threw aside his coat, jumped up, and came to Jesus. "What do you want me to do for you?" Jesus asked. "My rabbi," the blind man said, "I want to see!" And Jesus said to him, "Go, for your faith has healed you." Instantly the man could see, and he followed Jesus down the road (Mark 10:46-52, NLT).

Solomon intentionally sought God's attention. He might've been the king of Israel, but sacrificing 1,000 burnt offerings cost him something. God responded and asked, "What do you want? Ask, and I will give it to you!" Bartimaeus was persistent in trying to get Jesus' attention. Once he does, Jesus asks him, "What do you want me to do for you?" I believe that Jesus is asking us this same question: "What do you want me to do for you?"

We read books about discipleship, purity, and God's love. We hear sermons about being "all in," about being transformed into the image of Christ, and how we should take up the armor of God. But are we applying any of it to our lives in real, tangible ways? Maybe we take notes and look back at them a few months later. Maybe we're just hearing it and then walking out the door. I once spent several weeks reading a really good book written by a prominent pastor. I finished the 205-page book, closed it, and realized that I couldn't remember a single thing I'd read. The information was there, I definitely put the time into going through it, but I didn't take ownership of any it.

What are we holding onto that prevents us from being "all in"? Is it that important? Are we willing to stand before the Throne of God and try and explain it? "Well, God, I know you were calling me to be more, and I know that there were things I should do and needed to do. But, ya know, I just really couldn't stop _____. I just couldn't give up_____. It was just too hard! I'm sorry that I never loved my wife or my kids like I should but _____ was just too important to me so they had to wait. Yeah, I never did much of what You wanted me to do. Sorry about that. But we're still cool, right? I mean, You're gonna hook me up, right?"

It sounds stupid, doesn't it, but isn't that what we do? We ignore the strength Jesus offers in the face of our weakness, and when the Holy Spirit tries to counsel us, our response is, "Shut up. Go away." If we truly understood the God we serve, sin simply would *not* be an option.

> *The old sinful nature loves to do evil, which is just opposite from what the Holy Spirit wants. And the Spirit gives us desires that are opposite from what the sinful nature desires. These two forces are constantly fighting each other, and your choices are never free from this conflict. Those who belong to Christ Jesus have nailed the passions and desires of their sinful nature to his cross and crucified them there* (Galatians 5:17, 24, The Book).

> *And now that you have found God, why do you want to go back again and become slaves once more to the weak and useless spiritual powers of this world?* (Galatians 4:9, The Book)

> *As a dog returns to its vomit, so a fool repeats his folly* (Proverbs 26:11, The Book).

> *You have charged us to keep your commandments carefully. Oh that my actions would consistently reflect your principles! Then I will not be disgraced when I compare my life with your commands* (Psalm 119:4-6, The Book).

> *...I, the Lord, made you, and I will not forget to help you. I have swept away your sins like the morning mists. I have scattered your offenses like the clouds. Oh, return to me, for I have paid the price to set you free* (Isaiah 44:21-22, The Book).

We've come together for a reason. We could be doing a thousand other things right now, but we're not. We're here, seeking God's attention.

Discussion Questions

1. What is your response to God's question, "What do you want me to do for you?"

2. What is it you want from God?

3. What is preventing you from obtaining it?

✦3✦

Active Transformation

I have a confession to make. I've been doing a daily devotional, and I've been increasingly resentful of the "What will you do?" section. This part is intended to encourage me to internalize what I just read and make it part of me. Instead of doing that, I felt like, "Why do I have to be doing something? Can't I just meditate on this stuff?" It got bad enough that I actually rebelled and didn't fill it out for a while, until I realized how stupid this was.

Our spiritual transformation is a constant process requiring constant effort. So, if I'm not applying what I'm learning, if I'm not putting effort into my own transformation, what's the point of doing the devotional at all? What's the point of any of this? We've all heard the saying, "An object in motion tends to stay in motion." I hate to burst your bubble, but that's a lie. The truth is that unless energy or force is applied to an object, it will slow down, cease to move, and start decaying. It's not enough to want to be transformed. We have to actively participate in it. We have to do something.

Immediately after this, Jesus made his disciples get back into the boat and cross to the other side of the lake while he sent the people home. Afterward, he went up into the hills by himself to pray. Night fell while he was there alone. Meanwhile, the disciples were in trouble far away from land, for a strong wind had risen, and they were fighting heavy waves. About 3 o'clock in the morning Jesus came to them, walking on the water. When the disciples saw him, they screamed in terror, thinking he was a ghost. But Jesus spoke to them at once, "It's all right," he said. "I am here! Don't be afraid." Then Peter called to him, "Lord, if it's really you, tell me to come to you by walking on water." "All right, come," Jesus said. So Peter went over the side of the boat and walked on the water toward Jesus. But when he looked around at the high waves, he was terrified and began to sink. "Save me, Lord!" he shouted. **Instantly** *Jesus reached out his hand and grabbed him. "You don't have much faith" Jesus said. "Why did you doubt me?"* (Matthew 14:22-31, The Book, emphasis mine.)

Notice that Jesus waited for Peter to express a desire to get out of the boat and come to Him. Jesus could've called Peter out of the boat at any point, but what if Peter didn't want to go? What if Peter responded, "Nah—I'm good. Judas, you go!" Peter positions himself to be called forward by first seeking Jesus, who then summoned him. When Peter started to doubt, Jesus was there immediately, chastising in love and giving guidance for the future. ("You don't have much faith. Why did you doubt me?")

Later, Jesus asked His disciples, "Who do people say that the Son of Man is?" Simon Peter answered, "You are the Messiah, the Son of the living God." Jesus replied,

You are blessed, Simon son of John, because my Father in heaven has revealed this to you. You did not learn this from any human being. Now I say to you that you are Peter..." (Matthew 16:13, 16-18, The Book).

This is so powerful! Jesus, in effect, tells Peter, "Because you know who I am, I will tell you who you are."

Everyone who is victorious will eat of the manna that has been hidden away in heaven. And I will give to each one a white stone, and on the stone will be engraved a new name that no one knows except the one who receives it (Revelations 2:17, The Book)

Do you see the intimacy in this verse? Jesus tells us that He will give us a new name that only you and He will know! The name we were given at birth is not who we really are. When I was growing up, I knew a lady who was given her name because her dad really wanted a son. For her whole life, she carried a name that symbolizes the fact that her very existence was a disappointment to her father. But the name God has for her, for you and I, carries a power and a magnificence that declares who we really are! It is a name rooted in power and victory! Yes, Jesus sees the garbage in my life but He *knows* the person I am supposed to be. He designed, created, and purposed me for something. In order to find out what that is, in order to be that, I need to go see Him. I need to spend time with Him and get to know Him better. I need Him to tell me who I am and not rely on who I think I am.

We have to actively participate in our own transformation. We have to intentionally give Jesus access to the areas of our life that we still want to own and control. I know for me, if my ways were so good I would've ended up somewhere good. But, I didn't. I know for a fact that God's ways are so much better than mine. See, giving control of my life to Jesus isn't a bad thing. Jesus is *not* overbearing or domineering. I spent 20 years in the military, and I know what overbearing and controlling look and feel like. Jesus doesn't want to *take* control; He wants us to *give* control. When we do, He's gentle and loving in the way He leads us forward.

Discussion Questions

1. How are you applying things you read and hear towards your spiritual transformation?

2. How are you positioning yourself to be called forward by Jesus?

3. What area of life are you actively working to give God control of?

✦4✦

Kiddushin

In Matthew 21: 8-11, we read the story of Jesus' triumphant entry into Jerusalem. It says,

Most of the crowd spread their coats on the road ahead of Jesus, and others cut branches from the trees and spread them on the road. He was in the center of the procession, and the crowds all around him were shouting, "Praise God for the Son of David! Bless the one who comes in the name of the Lord! Praise God in highest heaven!" The entire city of Jerusalem was stirred as he entered. "Who is this?" they asked. And the crowds replied, "It's Jesus, the prophet from Nazareth in Galilee" (The Book).

Surely this had to seem like the high point in His public life to the disciples. The crowds had been getting bigger and following them all over the countryside. Jesus has performed miracle after miracle doing stuff they had never seen from the prophets of old. He fed thousands of people with some kid's sack lunch, He cast out demons, and raised people who were dead back to life. People were healed just by touching His clothes, and suddenly there's a massive parade and folks are shouting out His name and calling Him the king of Israel!

Then things start going sideways. Jesus goes to the temple and tears it up. He's hollering at people, kicking over tables, and throwing people out. Then He starts taking on the Pharisees and Sadducees and tells the crowds,

So practice and obey whatever (the teachers of religious law and the Pharisees) say to you, but don't follow their example. For they don't practice what they teach. They crush you with impos-

sible religious demands and never left a finger to help ease the burden. Everything they do is for show (Matthew 23:3-5, The Book)

Things don't really seem to settle down any. Jesus curses a fig tree—and it dies; He starts talking seriously about being betrayed and crucified; there's way more tension coming from the leading priests; some woman pours really expensive perfume all over Jesus, and their buddy Judas is starting to act kind of funny. All of this in just a few short days! Finally, the disciples get instructions from Jesus and go to prepare the Passover meal. I'm sure they were hoping that things would chill out, and they could catch a break from all the craziness of the past few days. We're all familiar with the following verses.

As they were eating, Jesus took a loaf of bread and asked God's blessing on it. Then he broke it in pieces and gave it to the disciples, saying, "Take it and eat it, for this is my body." And he took a cup of wine and gave thanks to God for it. He gave it to them and said, "Each of you drink from it, for this is my blood, which seals the covenant between God and his people" (Matthew 26:26-28, The Book).

I've heard that passage solemnly read at every Easter service and every time we had communion as I was growing up. I once heard about the various traditions and ceremonies from the Jewish culture of that time, and it totally changed my understanding and appreciation of that passage. It was all really interesting but the *Kiddushin* really jumped out at me.

Kiddushin is the first step in a two-step process. Kiddushin comes from the root word *Qof-Dalet-Shin*, which means sanctified. This ceremony set apart or dedicated the bride to the groom. From what I've read, the bride-to-be wasn't forced into the marriage. She was free to accept or decline the relationship. The ceremony was marked by a feast, and the bride and groom would share a cup of wine together to seal the relationship. From that moment on, the bride and groom were considered to be husband and wife although they were not allowed to live together until step 2, the *Nisu'in*, was completed. The groom would spend up to a year building a home where they would go to live once they were fully married. The time of separation was supposed to allow the deeper, spiritual connection between the two to fully develop.

As I thought about Jesus sharing a meal and a cup of wine with His disciples, and with us today through communion, as well as His words, "this…seals the covenant between God and his people." I was blown away. What I began to understand is that by participating in communion, I am publicly showing my dedication to Jesus Christ and declaring that I am set apart for a sacred purpose! Then I realized that even the practices of physical separation so that the spiritual connection is made strong and how the groom prepares a home for his bride is represented. Jesus said,

> There are many rooms in my Father's home, and I am going to prepare a place for you. If this were not so, I would tell you plainly. When everything is ready, I will come and get you, so that you will always be with me where I am (John 14:2-3, The Book)

We, as individuals, make up the church, and the church is frequently referred to in the New Testament as the "Bride of Christ." We are free to choose to be in a relationship with Jesus Christ. He has promised that He will always take care of us and will always be there for us. He promised that He's getting everything ready so we can be together forever and has sealed the relationship with His life.

I don't view communion as quite the solemn event where if my heart isn't right, then I'm going to get zapped somehow. While we participate in communion to commemorate Jesus' sacrifice, it's much more than that. We're also celebrating the fact that we are His. We don't deserve His love or His offer of a deeply intimate relationship, but clearly, He's offering it to us.

Discussion Questions

1. What do you think about the fact that God uses the fullness and intimacy of marriage to indicate the depth of the relationship He wants to have with us?

2. As a guy, how do you process the fact that we are the weaker person in our relationship with Christ?

3. In what ways are you learning to rely on God's strength and not your own?

⇒5⇐

Be a Godly Example

I know that I'm not the person I used to be. That's not the issue anymore. The issue is, "Am I different *today*?" Am I more submitted to Jesus Christ *today* than I was yesterday? Am I establishing a positive spiritual legacy in my home?

I know in my house we don't exactly have birds sitting on the windowsill chirping merry little tunes while we gladly do the dishes or fold laundry. There are times in my house when a life of faith looks a lot like me struggling not to lash out at one of the kids or the dog. So how can we demonstrate our faith? Is it playing gospel music; asking the kids, "Do you know Jesus loves you?" in syrupy tones; or saying, "Have a blessed day" instead of "goodbye"?

*And you must love the Lord your God with all your heart, all your soul, and all your strength. **And** you must commit your-selves wholeheartedly to these commands I am giving you today. Repeat them again and again to your children. Talk about them when you are at home and when you are away on a journey, when you are lying down and when you are getting up again* (Deuteronomy 6:5-7, NLT—emphasis mine).

Scottish philosopher Thomas Carlyle once said, "Conviction is worthless until it is converted to daily conduct." A more modern rendition might be, "Put up or shut up." We may feel strongly about things that go on in the world, but until we're ready to do something about them, all we're doing is adding to the noise sur-rounding whatever that issue happens to be. If we want to see a change in our homes, we have to demonstrate what that change should be. It can't be temporary or superficial. It has to be a true heart change.

15

In his first letter to Timothy, Paul says, "Be an example to all believers in what you say, in the way you live, in your love, your faith, and your purity" (1 Timothy 4:12, NLT).

I very much feel the pressure of being an example at home. What am I like on the way to church compared to how I am once I get there? What am I like when I come home from church or from men's group? Am I sorrowful and loving because God got ahold of me, or am I irritated and annoyed because He identified something in me that's not quite right? Am I different *today* compared to yesterday? Am I actually growing and changing in noticeable, measurable ways? That is what my family notices. I have to answer to God for the question, "Am I conducting myself, in every area of my life, in a way that pleases His heart?" We don't get to be leaders at home, leaders at work, or servant leaders at church unless we're first being led. We can't give away something we don't have or don't own. We can't teach something we don't know.

I've watched my daughter, who is now grown, learn how to roll over, crawl, walk, and talk. I've seen her personality develop and have watched as she discovered her talents. I remember her putting on skirts that were good twirlers, singing at the top of her lungs, saving earthworms from certain destruction as I worked in the garden. I have even let her do my hair so I could be "beautiful." I see her maturing and changing physically and emotionally. I know what she's capable of and just how awesome she is. I worry about her safety. I pray that she'll use wisdom and discernment as she makes decisions. I pray that she finds a young man who will see her, not just as a beautiful young lady, but as someone infinitely more interesting and beautiful inside. I pray he will treasure her as much as I do and will understand what a tremendous gift she is.

The thing is, I know my father-in-law feels the same way about his daughter. Am I treating my wife with the same tenderness and love that I want my daughter to receive from her husband? Am I making sure my wife knows she's valued and appreciated the way I want my daughter to be valued and appreciated? We teach people how to treat us by what treatment we accept from them. The way I treat my wife shows my daughter how she should expect to be treated. I'm casting the mold by which she'll choose a husband. This also applies to my son. He's learning from me how a man takes care of himself and how he talks to and treats a woman. He's learning how to be a father—from me! No pressure.

If you're like me, there are things from the family you were raised in that you don't want to carry forward into your family. Even if your childhood home life was idyllic, everyone puts a little bit different spin on their family because the structure is determined and defined by you and your wife. My wife and I have encountered things that neither one of us have a model for. I'm sure we could read some books on the subject, but the biggest influence in our lives, the thing that is actually making a difference, is our relationship with Jesus Christ.

Don't make your children angry by the way you treat them. Rather, bring them up with discipline and instruction approved by the Lord (Ephesians 6:4, The Book).

I once heard a pastor point out that the phrase, "bring them up" in the original Greek actually means that we are to nourish and feed our kids. Discipline isn't about punishment and control; it's about teaching and correcting in a way that Jesus would approve.

We can demonstrate that God is working in our life by *letting* God work in our life. He changes us from the inside out, and some changes take more time and effort than others. We need to stay submitted and ask for Him to purify us so we become the men that we were designed, created, and purposed to be. We need to love our family the way they need to be loved and not just how we know to do it, or worse yet cheat them by giving them leftovers. You get there by praying for each member of your family specifically. I promise that this will change how you see and feel about each one of them.

How can we be a better example in every area of our life? Is it about what we don't do, things we don't say, or places we don't go to? Or is it about how we conduct ourselves; by what we *do* say and how we say it? As a young man, I didn't have much interest in living a godly life, but I paid attention to those that did. The way they lived spoke louder to me than any sermon ever could. I was good friends with one family, and they were all athletic and outdoorsmen—avid hunters and fishermen. They were also incredibly funny! I remember how badly my sides ached from laughing after hanging out with them one evening. They weren't perfect, but they were pursuing more of Jesus Christ in their lives. Their example still stands out in my mind many decades later.

Who we are in Christ should be an ever-evolving realization. As we pursue Him, who we are changes as we conform more to His image. This isn't a cookie-cutter, one-size-fits-all situation. The ultimate goal is to become who *He* says we are—to be the one He designed, created, and purposed us to be.

Discussion Questions

1. How are you setting a godly example for your family?
2. How can you extend God's love to your wife and kids differently than how you have been?
3. If asked, would your wife and kids be able to honestly say that your relationship with Christ is making you a different man?

⇥6⇤

Dealing With Shame

I once heard it said that shame should only be connected to our sin until we deal with it. Shame is a barrier in our relationship with God. When Adam and Eve ate the fruit from the Tree of the Knowledge of Good and Evil, they broke the only rule God gave them.

Genesis 3:7 describes the immediate consequence of Eve and Adam eating of the forbidden fruit. It says, "At that moment, their eyes were opened, and they suddenly felt shame at their nakedness" (NLT).

The verses that follow describe how they attempted to cover their shame by stringing fig leaves together and then hid from God instead of going out to meet Him, as was their custom. When God asked them what was up, they didn't immediately confess their transgression. Adam blamed Eve, Eve blamed the serpent, and the serpent didn't care because he had accomplished his mission. He had successfully brought an end to the perfect relationship God had with those He had created.

I've often wondered about how Adam and Eve dealt with life after that. How many nights did they sit outside their cave, hut, teepee, or whatever, looking back towards the Garden, knowing they could never reenter it and regain that special relationship with God that they had lost? How many years did they sit there looking back at the Garden like that? How much did it hurt to stop doing it? I believe they eventually moved past shame and into regret.

We should not allow ourselves to get bogged down in shame. If shame is the result of sin in our life, and we keep choosing that sin, at some point we have to pick differently! I know I am tired of

19

circling around some of the same issues over and over again! If you think about it, it makes no sense to cooperate in any way, shape, or form with the very entity that's trying to kill you. Yet, when we deliberately go against what we know to be right and true, that's exactly what we're doing! That's so dumb!

Webster's Dictionary defines regret as, "to be very sorry for, an expression of distressing emotion." In the Old Testament, repent comes from the Hebrew word, *naham*[1] which means, "to change one's mind; be grieved." In the New Testament, repent comes from the Greek word, *metaneo*[2] which means, "to change any or all of the elements composing one's attitude, thoughts and behaviors concerning the demands of God for right living." We need to move from living a life with shame in it to living a life with regrets. Regret comes from repentance which drives us to God.

> *Tax collectors and other notorious sinners often came to listen to Jesus teach. This made the Pharisees and teachers of religious law complain that he was associating with such despicable people—even eating with them!* (Luke 15:1-2, The Book)

> *Matthew invited Jesus and his disciples to be his dinner guests, along with his fellow tax collectors and many other notorious sinners. The Pharisees were indignant. "Why does your teacher eat with such scum?" They asked his disciples. When he heard this, Jesus replied, "Healthy people don't need a doctor—sick people do. ...I have come to call sinners, not those who think they are already good enough"* (Matthew 9:10-13, The Book).

> *Jesus told this story... "Two men went to the Temple to pray. One was a Pharisee and the other was a dishonest tax collector. The proud Pharisee stood by himself and prayed this prayer: "I thank you, God, that I am not a sinner like everyone else, especially that tax collector over there! For I never cheat, I don't sin, I don't commit adultery, I fast twice a week and I give you a*

tenth of my income!" But the tax collector stood at a distance and dared not even lift his eyes to heaven as he prayed. Instead, he beat his chest in sorrow, saying, "O God, be merciful to me, for I am a sinner" " (Luke 18:10-13, The Book)

The Pharisee thought he had it figured out, had things covered, and was good to go. The tax collector knew he didn't have it all sorted out and was full of sorrow for the person he had become. He was so full of shame that he couldn't even raise his head to look towards heaven. The tax collector wanted to be different and moved in that direction. When you get around something that you just know will set you free, it is a powerful thing. When given that chance, you do what it takes to obtain your freedom, and you never forget what it took to get free.

We have to give up something in order to obtain what He has for us. It's not exactly an even trade though. It's more like handing over a poop-filled diaper and getting back keys to a brand new Porsche 911 Turbo. What we get in return far exceeds what we're giving up. What are we willing to let go of, what price are we willing to pay, in order to follow Jesus?

For me, it's letting go of the person I thought I was and the one whom I thought I wanted to be. The price I regularly pay is in pride and selfishness. Sometimes it's extremely difficult to make that payment—to do what's required of me when I have a choice to make. I can stick with what I've always done *or* I can step out, take up my cross, deny myself (cease to know whom I used to be), and follow Jesus.

Discussion Questions

1. What are you willing to let go of in order to follow Jesus?

2. What do you *need* to let go of (as opposed to being willing to let go of) in order to follow Jesus?

3. What is God pointing out in your life that you need to deal with?

---

[1] Strong's Concordance, Hebrew—5162
[2] Ibid, Greek—3340

✦ 7 ✦

Identity Crisis

We need to overcome the doubts that defeat us. We have to be careful of what we say to ourselves, about ourselves. How many times have we done something dumb and then said, "That's just what I always do." We need to stop condemning ourselves to a lesser life! That may be what we've always done, but we need to move past it. We need to start living the life God has for us to live and see ourselves as He does.

> *Truly I tell you, whatever you bind on earth will be bound in heaven, and whatever you loose on earth will be loosed in heaven* (Matthew 18:18, NIV).

I think the phrasing of that same passage in the "God's Word" translation is pretty powerful. "I can guarantee this truth: Whatever you imprison, God will imprison. And whatever you set free, God will set free."

God created each one of us and gave us strengths and weaknesses. Both are supposed to be used by Him and for Him. Our strengths point others to God. Our weaknesses point us to God. He knows us better than anyone or anything ever could. He loves us so much! He is full of grace and forgiveness, and has done everything He could possibly do to enable us to have a relationship with Him. In light of all this, it doesn't make much sense that we should give in to temptation instead of turning to Him.

> *Dear children, you belong to God. So you have won the victory over these people, because the one who is in you is greater than the one who is in the world* (John 4:4, GW).

As I was thinking about this earlier, I realized that my allowing an area of weakness to control my life is akin to allowing someone to rob me, taking my wallet, keys, and cell phone, when all they're holding is a water pistol while I've got a loaded .45 strapped on my hip! When I fall back to old behavior patterns because that's what I've always done, that's exactly what I'm doing! We have victory because of what Jesus has done. It's time to move on and leave all that other stuff behind.

I was watching a show about biker gangs, and one of the guys featured had been the Sergeant-at-Arms for the 1%ers. Now, the 1%ers are a particularly vicious bike club. Being a Sergeant-at-Arms for one of the chapters meant his job was to maintain order, function as a door and filter for initiates, and to be an internal enforcer. He'd done a lot of bad things and hurt a lot of people in the course of his time with the club. When he finally had enough and was allowed to "retire" from the club, he went home and burned his club patch, his colors, and all of his Harley Davidson t-shirts. He was done.

When Hernan Cortez started his expedition into the interior of the Yucatan peninsula, he burned the ships that got them there. This was a deliberate act on his part and reinforced the mentality that the only direction they had was forward. There was no other choice, and the only way to survive was to conquer and be victorious.

Jesus tells us, "Anyone who puts a hand to the plow and then looks back is not fit for the Kingdom of God" (Luke 9:62, The Book).

We need to be done with the past. We need to fix our eyes on the things God has for us to do and move forward into them. We all have areas that we struggle in. Yes, failure is part of working out our salvation, but it's not something we have to be okay with. Instead of accepting that "I always do this," FIGHT!

Therefore if you have been raised up with Christ, keep seeking the things above, where Christ is, seated at the right hand of

God. Set your mind on the things above, not on the things that are on earth. For you have died and your life is hidden with Christ in God (Colossians 3:1-3, NASB).

Does my definition of who I am line up with the person God says I am and the one He created me to be? Three things come to mind that we can do to move away from the person we think we are and to start taking on the person He knows us to be.

1. Pray. We need to ask God to show us who we are to Him and in Him.

2. Allow Him to redefine us. We have to participate in the process. We have to want it for ourselves!

3. Accept the changes He's trying to make in us. Be aware of what you say to yourself and make sure that it's aligned with His will, His vision, and His plan.

Discussion Questions

1. What things do you need to stop accepting as true about yourself that God never intended to be true about you?

2. What is God showing you about who He designed, created, and purposed you to be?

3. How are these things being made manifest in your life?

⇥8⇤

Disobedience

Have you ever considered that the only reason we've ever heard of Moses is that he obeyed God? It's true. I'd never really thought about that, but if you look at the beginning of his relationship with God, Moses didn't obey quickly or even willingly. He argued with God so much that Exodus 4:14 says God became angry with him. Eventually, Moses goes back home to announce that, like the Blues Brothers, He's "on a mission from God." Well...not quite. He goes back and asks his father-in-law for *permission* to return to Egypt to see his family. What? Okay, whatever. At least he's finally going in the right direction.

God gave him many assurances, signs, and even a helper, but Moses still balked. Why was it so hard for Moses to do what God was giving him to do? God was not asking us to deliver a message/warning to a ruthless dictator or walk around naked and barefoot as Isaiah did for three years. So, why do we resist doing what God is giving us to do? Is it because it's out of our comfort zone? Is it going to cost us something we'd rather not give up?

My father-in-law worked in construction his entire life. He started out digging ditches, became a roofer, and worked his way up to becoming a Project Manager building roads, aircraft hangers for the Navy, a natural gas refinery, and a chemical processing plant. As you can imagine, he's a physically tough, straightforward guy. When we would go over to my in-law's house for dinner, he'd usually cook something on the grill. At some point, the meat would end up in a pan and was sealed with foil so it could finish cooking. When everything was ready, he'd pull on a pair of welding gloves, grab the pan off the grill, and casually walk into the house.

One day he asked me to get the pan off the grill. No biggie, right? Wrong. I put on the welding gloves, grabbed the pan, and took exactly three steps before realizing how little protection those gloves offered! I also had no idea how calloused my father-in-law's hands were!

The longer we live in disobedience, the more we get used to it. Disobedience builds a callous on our heart. Before too long we don't hear the Holy Spirit trying to lead us anymore. That area of our life doesn't bother us—we're good with it.

All through the Bible, we're told of God's love for us and that He has wonderful plans for us—stuff we can't even imagine! All we have to do is obey Him.

> *Jesus called a small child over to him and put the child among them. Then he said, "I assure you, unless you turn from your sins and become as little children, you will never get into the Kingdom of Heaven"* (Matthew 18:2-3, The Book)

> *Jesus says "...Let the children come to me. don't stop them! For the Kingdom of God belongs to such as these"* (Mark 10:14, The Book)

> *Humans can reproduce only human life, but the Holy Spirit gives new life from heaven. So don't be surprised at my statement that you must be born again* (John 3:6-7, The Book).

See, spiritual growth is the exact opposite of physical growth. Physically, we are born pretty much helpless. Without someone to watch over us, feed and care for us, we'd die. We grow, mature, learn to fend for ourselves, and finally become independent enough to strike out on our own. Spiritually, we start out thinking that for the most part "we got this." We don't want to do what God tells us to do so we fight against Him. As we get to know Jesus and our relationship progresses, we find that we're still holding onto things that we shouldn't. After a lot of effort and needless suffering, we (hopefully) reach a point where we know that our efforts are pretty limited and choose to rely on Him more. The goal is to be totally surrendered and living in complete obedience.

I hope to reach a point where I hear and obey the first time He asks/tells me to do something. It takes work. It's hard. It costs us things about ourselves that we've come to believe as being true but were never supposed to be part of who we are—things that, frankly, we're okay with and really shouldn't be.

Discussion Questions

1. Why is it so important to hang onto _____ instead of turning it over to God?

2. There's always something in us being fed whenever we hang onto something that we shouldn't. What are you feeding?

3. What is God saying to you about how to move forward into a deeper relationship with Him?

✢9✢

The Story of Us

It was once said that "Sin causes us to shrink down to the size of ourselves." That's so true! Think about it. When it's all about you, and you become the center of your world, that's a pretty small place. Christianity isn't a *Power of Positive Thinking* kinda deal nor is it a belief that "I have the power of good in me" kind of mentality. Why? Because that's still about you! All that self-actualization nonsense is just that—nonsense. Nobody on this earth can lead you into a healing, growing, deeper relationship with Jesus Christ by teaching and encouraging you to seek your inner child then loving that tender innocence so that it grows into a peaceful coexistence with the universe. It ain't gonna happen!

Jesus addressed this kind of thinking when He said,

> *What good is it for one blind person to lead another? The first one will fall into a ditch and pull the other down also* (Luke 6:39, The Book).

> *If the light you think you have is really darkness, how deep that darkness will be* (Matthew 6:2-3 The Book).

We have to realize that this life is not about us. That's hard for me to accept some days, but that doesn't make it any less true. First Corinthians 6:19 tells us that our bodies were given to us by God, that we were bought at a high price! On Sunday mornings we sing songs declaring our love, our allegiance, that we are His, and so on, but do we understand what we're singing? Do we actually mean it, or are we worshipping Him with our lips and not our hearts?

The impact of just *one* man, who is dedicated to doing what God has for him to do, amazes me! Consider Noah. He built a massive boat, on dry land, during a time when there was no rain. Then he stocked it with supplies, loaded it down with animals, and closed the door. What about Paul the Apostle? He went from hunting down and imprisoning Christ-followers to planting churches. His letters to those churches comprise the bulk of the New Testament.

Now, if you're anything like me you're thinking, "That's cool. That's ancient history." But it's not! Look at Beth Moore who started out speaking at local events and is now a highly sought-after speaker with a *global* reach. Another example would be Robert Morris who founded Gateway Church in 2000 and now has eight locations with over 100,000 people in attendance.

Still thinking that this couldn't possibly be you? Okay, what about George Hobbs?

George Hobbs was the pastor of a small Christian Missionary Alliance church in northwestern PA in the 50s and 60s. By all accounts, he was very knowledgeable in God's Word. He was known as a real shepherd, caring for his congregation, and intentionally looking for those who desperately needed Jesus. His attitude was, "Get 'em saved—God will clean 'em up!" This definitely bucked the legalistic and exclusionary attitudes so prevalent in church society at that time.

When a nearby church was slated to be closed, he rearranged the services so he could preach at both churches and lead that congregation as well. George Hobbs died in the early 70s, leaving behind his wife and two children, a girl and a boy. The daughter would go on to a life of service to her mother and her own children who had serious physical challenges. She had a strong example of faith and dedication to follow, and she did not waver. George's son became a missionary to Indonesia where he founded a Bible college and spent over 20 years there, teaching and leading people to Jesus. He finally left Indonesia amid many threats on his life.

Another example is a young man who believed there was a

God but didn't know anything about Him. So, he read the Bible cover to cover. It was interesting, but you know—whatever. Then he was invited to a youth group meeting by some friends, got plugged in, and gave his life to Christ. Later he went on a mission trip and found purpose in what he was doing. That week-long mission trip turned into a month. When he finally went home, that young man packed up all of his stuff and drove back, much to the surprise of the missionary! He lived, served, and taught there, ultimately realizing that this is what he wanted to do with his life.

Every one of the people I just talked about connected with God's purpose for their life. They most likely did not have a grand vision for how things would go. No divine blueprints for starting a global ministry or a mega church were bestowed upon Beth Moore or Robert Morris. George Hobbs had no way of knowing the spiritual legacy he was establishing that now extends to a grandson, four granddaughters and ten great-grandchildren, all of whom are spending their lives on the mission field. And that young man...well, his story is still unfolding, but his impact is already being seen and felt in the church where he serves as a pastor.

Discussion Questions

1. You may not know the "big picture," but what is God asking you to do right now?

2. What is preventing you from connecting with your God-given purpose?

3. What would those closest to you (wife, family member, etc.) say is your biggest stumbling block?

✦10✦

Psalm 90

Psalm 90 is one of Moses' prayers, and when you read it, you can sense the depth of the relationship he had with God and the level of understanding he gained by it. It's only 17 verses (less than 280 words), and I want to share the whole thing with you. Listen to this!

Lord, through all the generations you have been our home! Before the mountains were created, before you made the earth and the world, you are God, without beginning or end. You turn people back to dust, saying, "Return to dust!" For you, a thousand years are as yesterday! They are like a few hours! You sweep people away like dreams that disappear or like grass that springs up in the morning. In the morning it blooms and flourishes, but by evening it is dry and withered. We wither beneath your anger; we are overwhelmed by your fury. You spread out our sins before you—our secret sins—and you see them all. We live our lives beneath your wrath. We end our lives with a groan. Seventy years are given to us! Some may even reach eighty. But even the best of these years are filled with pain and trouble; soon they disappear, and we are gone. Who can comprehend the power of your anger? Your wrath is as awesome as the fear you deserve. Teach us to make the most of our time, so that we may grow in wisdom. O Lord, come back to us! How long will you delay? Take pity on your servants! Satisfy us in the morning with your unfailing love so we may sing for joy to the end of our lives. Give us gladness in proportion to our former misery! Replace the evil years with good. Let us see your miracles again; let our children see your glory at work. And may the

Lord our God show us his approval and make our efforts successful. Yes, make our efforts successful! (Psalm 90, The Book)

I think we could spend a long time dissecting this prayer, but there are a couple things I want to touch on. First, in verse 8 it says, "You spread out our sins before you—our secret sins—and you see them all." When I read that, I was reminded of Hebrews 4:12-13,

> *For the word of God is full of living power. It is sharper than the sharpest knife, cutting deep into our innermost thoughts and desires. It exposes us for what we really are. Nothing in all creation can hide from him. Everything is naked and exposed before his eyes. **This** is the God to whom we must explain all that we have done* (The Book, emphasis mine).

Sin only has power in our life if we allow it to. As long as you think something is okay, then it is! I know the only time I'm able to start moving past something is when I decide that whatever I'm struggling with is no longer acceptable. It sounds simple, but it's a huge step! By admitting and actually stating that something is wrong, we begin to break the spiritual agreement that we made. This isn't the same thing as knowing that something is wrong, and we shouldn't be doing whatever or acting a certain way. We *must* decide that what we're doing is no longer tolerable.

Secondly, verse 12 says, "Teach us to number our days, that we may gain a heart of wisdom." Moses is talking about making each day count for something. Remember Tim McGraw's song, "Live like you were dying"? The dying man in the song shared some of the things that he learned. The greatest lesson was to deeply love and treat kindly the people who mattered most in his life and to let go of unforgiveness. I think for most guys, that's where it hits hard.

Growing up in a Pennsylvania steel town when I did meant that guys didn't articulate their feelings and rarely showed emotion. I'm not whining about it now, but I want more for my kids. I want my kids to know that I love them, that I'm proud of them, and so I tell them these things all the time. I also tell them that God has amazing things planned for them that only they are supposed to do. It's not just words; I believe it for them just as I believe it for myself and for you.

I believe gaining "a heart of wisdom" comes from being close to God. Psalm 86:11 says, "Teach me your ways, O Lord, that I may live according to your truth! Grant me purity of heart, that I may honor you" (The Book).

My personal life prayer comes out of that scripture. I truly want to walk in His ways and have His heart overlay mine so my life honors Him. I want people to see Jesus, not me and not in a "hiding behind" way (don't look at me—look at Jesus!) but more along the lines of when your son/daughter copies you and your wife says, "You're just like your Dad!"

God paid a high price for you, so don't be enslaved by the world (1 Corinthians 7:23, NLT).

I remember Depeche Mode had a song out in the early 90s, "Get Right With Me." The song talks about how we would value our life differently if we had to buy it. That always stuck out to me as being true. If your life were a commodity sitting on the shelf, would you buy it or would you put it back? I want my life to count for something. I want Jesus to be proud of me. I want to hear the words, "Well done, good and faithful servant!" spoken to me and to feel the warmth of His smile as He says them.

Discussion Questions

1. What part of you still has permission to be there even though you know it no longer should be?

2. How has God been refining you recently?

3. How would you define the current status of your relationship with God?

❖11❖

Worship

Worship, as used in the Bible, is a verb. It's something we do. It's not just the "singy" part of a service; it should be part of our daily life. Worship begins and ends with God—it's about Him. Listen to Psalm 139:

*O Lord, you have examined my heart and know everything about me. You know when I sit down or stand up. You know my every thought when far away. You chart the path ahead of me and tell me where to stop and rest. Every moment you know where I am. You know what I am going to say even before I say it, Lord. You both precede **and** follow me. You place your hand of blessing on my head. Such knowledge is too wonderful for me, too great for me to know! I can never escape from your spirit! I can never get away from your presence!*

If I go up to heaven, you are there; if I go down to the place of the dead, you are there. If I ride the wings of the morning, if I dwell by the farthest oceans, even there your hand will guide me, and your strength will support me. I could ask the darkness to hide me and the light around me to become night—but even in the darkness, I cannot hide from you. To you, the night shines as bright as day. Darkness and light are both alike to you.

You made all the delicate inner parts of my body and knit me together in my mother's womb. Thank you for making me so wonderfully complex! Your workmanship is marvelous—and how well I know it. You watched me as I was being formed in utter seclusion, as I was woven together in the dark of the womb. You saw me before I was born. Every day of my life was recorded in your book. Every moment was laid out before a single day had passed. How precious are your thoughts about me, O God! They are innumerable! I can't even count them; they outnumber the grains of sand! And when I wake up in the morning, you are still with me! Search me, O God, and know my heart; test me and know my thoughts. Point out anything in me that offends you, and lead me along the path of everlasting life (The Book, emphasis mine).

Now *that* is a man worshipping and praising his Creator and God! It's true that our obedience reflects where we are in our relationship with Jesus, but our worship reflects where we are too.

Look at the Old Testament prophet Isaiah. He lived through the civil war between the tribes of Israel after Solomon died. He watched the nation devolve into idol worship and, as a prophet, delivered pointed messages from God to people who didn't want to hear about it. He saw Israel destroyed by the Assyrians yet in Isaiah 61:10 he says,

I am overwhelmed with joy in the Lord my God! For he has dressed me in the clothing of salvation and draped me in a robe of righteousness. I am like a bridegroom in his wedding suit or a bride with her jewels (The Book).

Isaiah talks about the "clothing of salvation" and a "robe of righteousness," which are not physically seen, and compares them with a groom wearing his best suit and the bride adorned in her finest jewelry.

I remember the day I got married. I barely ate, and what I did eat, I couldn't taste. I obliterated every posted speed limit just so I could get to the church almost three hours too early. When I saw my soon-to-be wife at the top of the aisle, my entire being was flooded with powerful emotions. Isaiah is associating the anticipation, the excitement, and the promise of one of the biggest days in someone's life to something God has given him.

Isaiah is a man who suffered the scorn and indignities that come with telling your people and nation that they're going to be conquered and led away into captivity. Yet here he is expressing joy, excitement, and anticipation, like one experiences on their wedding day, as part of his relationship with God!

We need to live with a sense of anticipation and expectation when it comes to our relationship with God. I've got a couple quick examples to help explain what I mean.

Anticipation: I look forward to my devotional time. It settles and quiets my soul like nothing else. As soon as I slide into my favorite chair and grab my Bible, I generally relax and am able to focus on what God has for me. I genuinely look forward to men's group, even though I have to get up early to be there.

Expectation: I believe that no matter how many times I read through the Bible, God will bring it to life differently each time. God always shows me what I need to know and understand as I read His Word. I know that the guys who show up to men's group expect that they'll be challenged to grow in their faith.

We need to approach our relationship with God with a sense of anticipation and expectation because He loves us more than we can possibly imagine. He will always care for us and lead us forward. We need to deliberately spend time worshipping Him and expressing joy and gratitude for all He's done.

Discussion Questions

1. When you sit down and enter into worship or have devotional time, do you expect to meet with God?

2. Do you expect He has something to say to you or show you during these times?

3. Do you look forward to your devotional or worship time?

⇥12⇤

Jesus Ain't Your Hobby

Jesus taught using parables, but He also spoke very plainly and told us what it costs to follow Him.

Great crowds were following Jesus. He turned around and said to them, "If you want to be my follower you must love me more than your own father and mother, wife and children, brothers and sisters—yes, more than your own life. Otherwise, you cannot be my disciple. And you cannot be my disciple if you do not carry your own cross and follow me. But don't begin until you count the cost. For who would begin construction of a building without first getting estimates and then checking to see if there is enough money to pay the bills? Otherwise, you might complete only the foundation before running out of funds. And then how everyone would laugh at you! They would say, "There's the person who started building and ran out of money before it was finished!" Or what king would ever dream of going to war without first sitting down with his counselors and discussing whether his army of ten thousand is strong enough to defeat the twenty thousand soldiers who are marching against him? If he is not able, then while the enemy is still far away, he will send a delegation to discuss terms of peace. So no one can become my disciple without giving up everything for me (Luke 14:25-33, The Book).

Jesus is not a hobby. We can't pick Him up like we do a guitar. We can't "do church" and think we've got the "spiritual thing" covered. We have to be honest in our assessment of who we are and where we're at. We have to seek Him out and be intentional in building the relationship. We need to rely on His strength and wisdom when attacking the things in life that are trying to keep us in bondage. We simply can't do it by ourselves.

"Why do your disciples disobey our age-old traditions" (the Pharisees) demanded. "They ignore our tradition of ceremonial hand washing before they eat." Jesus replied, "And why do you, by your traditions, violate the direct commandments of God?" (Matthew 15:1-3, The Book)

The Pharisees were bent out of shape because Jesus' disciples didn't perform ritualistic hand washing before eating. Jesus chastised the Pharisees for being "religious" and went straight after the heart issue. He quotes Isaiah saying of the Pharisees,

These people honor me with their lips, but their hearts are far away. Their worship is a farce, for they replace God's commands with their own man-made teachings.

Then He calls out to the crowd,

Listen to what I say and try to understand. You are not defiled by what you eat; you are defiled by what you say and do (Matthew 15:8-11, The Book).

Later, Peter asks for more of an explanation and Jesus tells him,

Anything you eat passes through the stomach and then goes out of the body. But evil words come from an evil heart and defile the person who says them. For from the heart come evil thoughts, murder, adultery, all other sexual immorality, theft, lying, and slander. THESE are what defile you (Matthew 15:15 -20, The Book, emphasis mine).

James reinforces this point in chapter 1, verses 13-16,

And remember, no one who wants to do wrong should ever say, "God is tempting me." God is never tempted to do wrong, and he never tempts anyone else either. Temptation comes from the lure of our own evil desires. These evil desires lead to evil actions, and evil actions lead to death (The Book).

The flip side of that is given to us in 2 Peter 1:3-9. Skipping to verse 5 it says,

Your faith will produce a life of moral excellence. A life of moral excellence leads to knowing God better. Knowing God leads to self-control. Self-control leads to patient endurance, and patient endurance leads to godliness. Godliness leads to love for other Christians, and finally you will grow to have genuine love for everyone (The Book).

Notice how Peter walks us in. It's not just a logical progression, it's how a relationship develops.

Paul talks about God's eternal kingdom and says,

Against its will, everything on earth was subjected to God's curse. All creation anticipates the day when it will join God's children in glorious freedom from death and decay (Romans 8:20-21, The Book).

When Adam and Eve decided to believe a lie and pursue their own desires instead of following God's instructions to them, they condemned you and I to live in this sinful world. We have no say in it whatsoever; we're stuck with their choice. But, before I get all uptight about them, am I any better? Would I have walked away from temptation and sin, choosing my relationship with God instead? On a good day I might have a shot at getting it right, but I also know that I can be incredibly weak. To be honest, I sometimes struggle to put away the chips and dip so I definitely can't get too judgmental here.

Choosing God's will and way over mine takes work. There's just no way around that. There are times when we will have to deliberately, forcibly, make ourselves go against what our sin-nature wants. The "all in" commitment stated in Deuteronomy 6:5 is the standard, and Jesus reiterated that fact. There's not been any lessening of those requirements. If anything, we have less of an excuse now than what the Israelites did once they were set free from slavery in Egypt. Whereas they had a massive set of laws, festivals, and practices to adhere to, Jesus made it possible for us to have a direct relationship with God.

When it comes to disciplining our kids, my wife and I have sought to address the heart issue behind whatever transgression they've committed. There's a physical consequence to their actions, but the most important part for us is helping them realize the "why" behind their actions. Once that heart motive has been identified, it can be properly addressed.

God treats us the same way. He gave everything and did everything there is to do so we can have a relationship with Him. Through that relationship He can love on us more. He'll help us identify the "why" behind our actions and then lead us into healing and restoration. Our relationship with Jesus is *not* a hobby. It's a lifelong partnership with someone who knows us best and loves us most.

Discussion Questions

1. Are you pursuing Jesus like you truly need Him or are you just putting in some time?

2. What heart issue is God addressing within you?

3. Does recognizing sin as a heart issue change how you address it?

→13←

Pastel Jesus

I think people are comfortable with the thought of Jesus loving them and announcing them before the Father as belonging to Him. However, it's much less comfortable to consider that we will be judged by Him and possibly sentenced to destruction. I believe most people are less threatened by what I call the "Pastel Jesus." You know what I'm talking about—the tender guy portrayed in pictures that looks serene, has soft features, and is holding a lamb in His arms.

It's easy to picture Jesus kind of breezing through the Holy Land, healing people, casting out demons, and telling people that their sins are forgiven. It's much tougher to consider that He lived with the Jewish leadership actively trying to ensnare and kill Him or that He had to manage large crowds of people that had their own ideas and agenda for Him as their Messiah.

Jesus went against societal norms by actually touching a leper in order to heal him. Jesus healed people on the Sabbath and felt utter contempt for the religious spirit of the Pharisees who would've ignored the person's suffering instead of setting them free. Can you imagine seeing the fire in His eyes as He cleared the money changers and merchants out of the temple with a whip? When the chief priests openly challenge Jesus' authority, He refused to answer them. Jesus was anything but "pastel."

You must love the Lord your God with all your heart, all your soul, and all your strength (Deuteronomy 6:5, The Book).

Easy stuff, right? Yeah, sure. When was the last time any of us gave 100% of ourselves mentally, emotionally, physically, and spiritually to anything? Unless we've been in a life-threatening situation at some point, it's not likely that any of us have. Yet, for God, this is Rule #1! If you pause to consider what's being asked, you'll realize that there's no way to do this on our own.

Even Jesus said it was humanly impossible. In Mark 10 we are given the story of the rich man who asked Jesus what he needed to do to gain eternal life.

As Jesus started on his way, a man ran up to him and fell on his knees before him. "Good teacher," he asked, "what must I do to inherit eternal life?" "Why do you call me good?" Jesus answered. "No one is good—except God alone. You know the commandments: "You shall not murder, you shall not commit adultery, you shall not steal, you shall not give false testimony, you shall not defraud, honor your father and mother.""
"Teacher," he declared, "all these I have kept since I was a boy." Jesus looked at him and loved him. "One thing you lack," he said. "Go, sell everything you have and give to the poor, and you will have treasure in heaven. Then come, follow me." At this the man's face fell. He went away sad, because he had great wealth (Mark 10:17-22, NIV).

After receiving the answer he hoped not to hear, the guy shuffles off and Jesus says to His disciples, "How hard it is for rich people to get into the Kingdom of God!" This amazed them. But Jesus said again,

Dear children, it is very hard to get into the Kingdom of God. It is easier for a camel to go through the eye of a needle than for a rich person to enter the Kingdom of God!" The disciples were astounded. "Then who in the world can be saved?" they asked. Jesus looked at them intently and said, "Humanly speaking, it is impossible. But not with God. Everything is possible with God" (Mark 10:23-2, The Book).

Jesus wasn't here to be all peaceful like Gandhi. He was here to bring the battle directly *to* Satan.

Don't imagine that I came to bring peace to the earth! No, I came to bring a sword. I have come to set a man against his father, and a daughter against her mother, and a daughter-in-law against her mother-in-law. Your enemies will be right in your own household! If you love your father or mother more than you love me, you are not worthy of being mine; or if you love your son or daughter more than me, you are not worthy of being mine. If you cling to your life, you will lose it; but if you give it up for me, you will find it (Matthew 10:34-39, The Book).

Can you imagine being in the crowd when Jesus said this? We read this stuff, but do we take the time to put ourselves in the scene and consider the context of what's being said? The people there that day had "Thou shalt honor thy father and thy mother" ingrained into their culture. Yet here's Jesus saying that unless you love *Him* more than your father and mother, you're not worthy. I imagine that the people in the crowd were thinking, "Wait, I thought you might be the Messiah, but you're saying that *you* are more important than my mom and dad? This doesn't make sense to me!" We have to make sure that our perception of Jesus lines up with the reality of who He is.

For the word of God is full of living power. It is sharper than the sharpest knife, cutting deep into our innermost thoughts and desires. It exposes us for what we really are. Nothing in all creation can hide from him. Everything is naked and exposed before his eyes. This is the God to whom we must explain all that we have done (Hebrews 4:12-13, The Book).

We will stand before Jesus and be judged, not just for our actions but for our heart motive behind those actions—the real reason behind doing what we did. Contrary to popular stories and jokes, Saint Peter won't be at the Pearly Gates. There won't be anyone there that we can hope to reason with, talk things through, or schmooze. It will be Jesus, in all of His power and glory coming in and taking His place on the throne. At that moment, everyone will know they don't deserve to be there and will wish they could crawl under something and pull a mountain over top of them to try and hide.

Jesus is God's Son and, make no mistake, we're either serving Him or we're not. God made the criteria for holiness and righteousness very plain. In Jesus, He provided a matchless example that it can be done, and He provided the way to have a relationship with Himself. Jesus conquered every temptation, every emotion, and even conquered death itself. He now sits at the right hand of the Father and is offering us wisdom, guidance, healing, forgiveness, and freedom. "This is the God to whom we must explain all that we have done."

Discussion Questions

1. Do you ever consider what it will be like to stand before Jesus and be judged?

2. What do you think about when you hear/read Hebrews 4:12-13?

3. How do you feel about Jesus saying that we must love Him more than our wife and kids?

✦14✦

Joshua 24

Joshua was commissioned by God to lead the nation of Israel into the Promised Land. He has been their leader for roughly 40-50 years and was a trusted, revered, aging warrior. Joshua knew his time was getting short, and he called all of the people together for this sort of a history class meets William Wallace moment.

This is what the Lord, the God of Israel, says: Your ancestors, including Terah, the father of Abraham and Nahor, lived beyond the Euphrates River, and they worshiped other gods. But I took your ancestor Abraham from the land beyond the Euphrates and led him into the land of Canaan. I gave him many descendants through his son Isaac. To Isaac I gave Jacob and Esau. To Esau I gave the hill country of Seir, while Jacob and his children went down into Egypt.

Then I sent Moses and Aaron, and I brought terrible plagues on Egypt, and afterward I brought you out as a free people. But when your ancestors arrived at the Red Sea, the Egyptians chased after you with chariots and horses. When you cried out to the Lord, I put darkness between you and the Egyptians. I brought the sea crashing down on the Egyptians, drowning them. With your very own eyes you saw what I did. Then you lived in the wilderness for many years.

Finally, I brought you into the land of the Amorites on the east side of the Jordan. They fought against you, but I gave you victory over them, and you took possession of their land. Then Balak son of Zippor, king of Moab, started a war against Israel. He asked Balaam son of Beor to curse you, but I would *not listen to him. Instead, I made Balaam bless you, and so I rescued you from Balak. When you crossed the Jordan River and came to Jericho, the men of Jericho fought against you. There were also many others who fought you, including the Amorites, the Perizites, the Canaanites, the Hittites, the Girgashites, the Hivites, and the Jebusites. But I gave you victory over them. And I sent hornets ahead of you to drive out the two kings of the Amorites. It was **not** your swords or bows that brought you victory. I gave you land you had not worked for, and I gave you cities you did not build—the cities in which you are now living. I gave you vineyards and olive groves for food, though you did not plant them.*

So honor the Lord and serve him wholeheartedly. Put away forever the idols your ancestors worshipped when they lived beyond the Euphrates River and in Egypt. Serve the Lord alone. But if you are unwilling to serve the Lord, then chose today whom you will serve. Would you prefer the gods your ancestors served beyond the Euphrates? Or will it be the gods of the Amorites in whose land you now live? But as for me and my family, we will serve the Lord.

The people replied, "We would never forsake the Lord and worship other gods. For the Lord our God is the one who rescued us and our ancestors from slavery in the land of Egypt. He performed mighty miracles before our very eyes. ...we are determined to serve the Lord!"

"You are accountable for this decision," Joshua said. Y"ou have chosen to serve the Lord. "Yes" (the people) replied, "we are accountable." "All right then," Joshua said, "destroy the idols among you..." (Joshua 24:2-17, 21-23, The Book, emphasis mine).

God reminded them of where they came from. He reminded them of all the things He had done to protect them and of the gifts

He's given them. Then they were presented with, "Honor and serve the Lord alone. Or would you prefer the gods your ancestors served? What about the gods of the people you just conquered and now live in their houses? You get to choose." I love how Joshua drives it home! "The very thing you worship in private, that thing you do in secret and hold dear to your heart even though you know it's displeasing to God—**get rid of it**. You're accountable for your decision."

Paul tells us to, "Set your minds on things above, not on earthly things" (Colossians 3:2, The Book). The King James reads, "Set your **affections** on things above…" (emphasis mine).

We're to set our focus, intent, will, desires, love, and devotion on what matters to God. This is the only way to attain the life He has for us. Our Christian walk isn't about what we can't do or things we shouldn't have in our lives. It's about what Jesus is offering us. It's an empowering, freeing life, full of challenges, trials, sacrifice, and obedience, and it is the most amazing and rewarding undertaking we can ever aspire to.

It's not enough to have had *an* encounter with Jesus. That's everyone's starting point, but that's not the ending! We have to constantly press forward. God reminded the nation of Israel of all that He had done for them, yet they still had idols in their lives. They were given a choice to either move forward into all that God had for them or continue to cling to their idols. Then, they were given full ownership of that decision.

If we want more, we have to be bold enough to ask for it *and* be willing to follow it through. If we're not being drawn closer to Jesus, it's not His fault—it's ours. Do we ever take an honest look at ourselves and say, "Lord Jesus, I need so much more of You in my life! Please—fill me anew! I want to be the man You died to save. Purify me, Lord." If not, why?

Discussion Questions

1. Where is God giving you victory in your life?

2. What are you holding onto that you need to let go of?

3. How do you avoid letting something become an idol in your life?

→15←

Ruth

Don't ask me to leave you and turn back. I will go wherever you go and live wherever you live. Your people will be my people, and your God will be my God. I will die where you die and will be buried there. May the Lord punish me severely if I allow anything but death to separate us! (Ruth 1:16-17, NLT)

These words were spoken by a young widow, Ruth, to her aging mother-in-law, Naomi. Naomi was going home after losing her husband and two sons. She was going back to where she grew up and still had family. Ruth, on the other hand, was leaving her family and the land where she'd grown up. She was leaving her culture and moving to another country whose people didn't like her people.

Ruth felt strongly about going with Naomi. She certainly didn't have to do it, given that Naomi had released her daughters-in-law and told them to go back to their own families. When they protested, Naomi was upfront with them about their situation, and one of them left. Ruth stayed. Why? Her sister-in-law was going home, and it would've been easy for her to go too, but she didn't. We may not know why Ruth felt so strongly about staying with Naomi, but we do know that Ruth positioned herself to be a blessing and to be blessed by God.

Ruth 2 tells us that Naomi and Ruth arrived in Bethlehem at the beginning of the barley harvest. I imagine they spent a little bit of time finding a place to stay, unpacking, and setting up the house. Afterward, Ruth volunteered to go out into the fields and try to gather some food. This was a risky undertaking for her. Ruth was a foreigner, a young woman with no family, no husband and no male protector. She was potentially risking her purity and her life by doing this. She didn't go out looking for someone to take notice of her and want to marry her. She didn't ask Naomi to arrange another marriage or find someone in the family to take care of them. Ruth decided that they need to fend for themselves and then went about doing just that.

She ended up working in the fields of someone who could directly impact Ruth and Naomi's life—Boaz. Boaz came from Bethlehem to check on how the harvest was going, noticed Ruth, and asked who she was. His foreman told him that Ruth was the woman who came back with Naomi and she had been working hard all day except for a few minutes rest. Boaz told Ruth to stay in his fields and to stick close to the ladies who were working for him. He assured her that nobody would bother her and to help herself to water others had drawn out of the well.

When Ruth asked Boaz why he was being so kind to her, he replies,

> *I know about the love and kindness you have shown your mother-in-law since the death of your husband. I have heard how you left your father and mother and your own land to live here among complete strangers. May the Lord, the God of Israel, under whose wings you have come to take refuge, reward you fully* (Ruth 2:11-12, NLT, emphasis mine).

Ruth's sacrifice and dedication did not go unnoticed. Her coming to town with Naomi was a big deal. I'm sure everyone watched her and paid attention to the way she cared for her mother-in-law. The foreman certainly noticed her work ethic. I love it that she was doing what she seemed to feel in her heart she should do, and God provided protection and blessing over her life.

Ruth stayed with Naomi and worked hard picking up crops that other people had dropped. They lived off of what others cast off. She wasn't too proud to do what needed to be done in order to provide for them. She was a woman of strength, a woman of character. In the end, Boaz arranged to marry her, and I think he counted himself fortunate to have her as his wife. But why? He was a rich man and probably could've married anyone he desired. I believe it's because of who she was. It matters who you partner with; who you align yourself with.

Ruth heard from God and was led by Him. That's why she chose to stay with Naomi and how she ended up working in Boaz's fields. Hearing and listening are not the same thing. Ruth *listened* to God. We need to practice listening to God. I say "practice" because how many times do we get a random thought and dismiss it (because it's random!) only to see later that God was trying to tell us something?

I have a motorcycle and really enjoy riding it. This might sound odd, but I pray about whether or not I should take it out. One time we had a week of cold, wet weather, and it was supposed to be beautiful the next day. I thought it would be great to ride into work, so that night I asked God if I should do so and felt like He was saying I should drive my car instead. That's not really the answer I was looking for. Admittedly, I asked Him again in the morning, hoping that He'd change His mind, but that didn't happen. So, I drove the car.

Now, I don't always get to see or understand the "why" behind His leading, but this day He showed me. There's a corner that I generally look forward to. I usually go into it with a fair amount of speed, roll on the throttle, and come out of it pretty hot. I love it! I drove the car, and as I got to my favorite corner, there was a big gravel spill covering the road. This is what's known as "the opposite of a good thing." Making it worse is that the gravel spill was in a spot that I couldn't see when I entered that corner. I could feel the car slide across the lane as I hit the gravel. Had I been on the bike, I would've been badly hurt. It was a stark reminder of why I need to follow His leading even when it runs contrary to my desires.

I can't say that I always ask God about the things I should or that I always listen. But we need to position ourselves to hear from Him. We need to practice hearing His voice. We need to pay attention to what it feels like when He speaks. We need to *expect* to hear from Him! When we do hear His voice, we need to listen (versus just "hearing") and obey. As demonstrated by Ruth, we have no idea what the outcome of our obedience will be.

Discussion Questions

1. Do you expect to hear from God as you go about your day?

2. When was the last time God told you to do something?

3. What does obedience to the leading of the Holy Spirit look like for you?

→16←

2 Kings 5

In 2 Kings 5 we read about Naaman's journey from being a prideful battlefield commander to a man that has a heart change and knows that there is only one God. But, there's also another story being told, and that's the story of Gehazi.

Gehazi was Elisha's servant. He'd been with Elisha for a long time, had witnessed many of the miracles performed, and had seen Elisha boldly deliver messages from God. For instance, 2 Kings 3 tells about the time when God promised through Elisha that the kings of Israel and Judah would defeat the Moabites. Second Kings 4 recounts how oil was provided to a widow so she could rescue her two sons from creditors who were going to take them as slaves, how a barren woman was given a promise that she would have a son, how God used Elisha to bring that boy back to life after he died, how poisonous stew was made safe to eat, and how 20 loaves of bread miraculously fed 100 men. Gehazi had witnessed all of these things.

As Elisha's servant, he would've been privy to much more than what's recorded in the Bible, but *he was there* for all of it! Now Elisha had been Elijah's attendant and asked to become his successor in the same manner as a first born son. It's possible that Gehazi could have been similarly positioned. Ultimately, he received a curse that extended to his family line forever. Why? What happened? Naaman.

Naaman was the commander of the Aramean army and was held in high regard by the king of Aram because he was very skilled and proficient. Unfortunately, Naaman had leprosy. He's told that there's a prophet in Samaria who could cure him and, after obtaining permission and a letter of introduction from the king, Naaman sets off to see Elisha. As commander of the army, Naaman would've directed bands of Arameans to conduct raids on Israel. Undoubtedly people were killed, others were taken as slaves, and what wasn't burned was plundered. So, when *the guy* who's responsible for a lot of bad things happening to Israel shows up asking to be healed, it undoubtedly was a tough moment.

Naaman and his entourage show up at Elisha's house, and a messenger is sent out with instructions on what he must do to be cured of leprosy.

Naaman went away angry and said, "I thought that he would surely come out to me and stand and call on the name of the Lord his God, wave his hand over the spot and cure me of my leprosy. Are not Abana and Pharpar, the rivers of Damascus, better than all the waters of Israel? couldn't I wash in them and be cleansed?" So he turned and went off in a rage. Naaman's servants went to him and said, "My father, if the prophet had told you to do some great thing, would you not have done it? How much more, then, when he tells you, 'Wash and be cleansed!'" So he went down and dipped himself in the Jordan seven times, as the man of God had told him, and his flesh was restored and became clean like that of a young boy. Then Naaman and all his attendants went back to the man of God. He stood before him and said, "Now I know that there is no God in all the world except in Israel" (2 Kings 5:11-15, NIV).

If advising Naaman on what he must do in order to be healed instead of cursing him wasn't bad enough, what pushed Gehazi over the edge was Elisha's refusal to accept any of the 750 pounds of silver, 150 pounds of gold, or any of the 10 sets of what were likely to be really nice clothes.

After Naaman had traveled some distance, Gehazi, the servant of Elisha the man of God, said to himself, "My master was too easy on Naaman, this Aramean, by not accepting from him what he brought. As surely as the Lord lives, I will run after him and get something from him (2 Kings 5:19-20, NIV).

Notice the anger, hatred, and greed? He even brought God into his disobedience by saying, "As surely as the Lord lives..." This had nothing to do with God; this was all about Gehazi. He chased Naaman down and made up a story about a couple young prophets coming to town, and although Elisha doesn't want anything for himself, he would like to ask for a couple things for them. Naaman is happy to oblige and encourages him to take two bags of silver. I can hear Gehazi feigning sheepishness and saying, "Okay, well.... if you insist, I'll take two bags of silver. It's for the young prophets, after all."

Now, bear in mind that Gehazi was a servant, but Naaman showed honor to him because of his master and sent a couple guys to carry the silver for Gehazi. They stopped short of town, and he thanked the guys for being so helpful and then hid the stuff in his house. He went back to Elisha and *lied* about where He'd been. This guy was *not* the sharpest knife in the drawer. He was lying to Elisha—a prophet!

When Gehazi came to the hill, he took the things from the servants and put them away in the house. He sent the men away and they left. When he went in and stood before his master, Elisha asked him, "Where have you been, Gehazi?" "Your servant didn't go anywhere," Gehazi answered. But Elisha said to him, "Was not my spirit with you when the man got down from his chariot to meet you?" (2 Kings 5:24-26, NIV)

"Do you think I don't know where you've been and what you've done?" I can't imagine the sinking feeling Gehazi had in the pit of his stomach. Because of his deception, his refusal to admit what he'd done, and the things he was harboring in his heart, Gehazi inherited Naaman's leprosy. I find it ironic. He so badly wanted what Naaman had, and he got it.

Both men were forever changed at the end of this story. Naaman started out as an enemy and was almost too proud to do what it took to be made whole. He left with his heart changed knowing that, "There is no God in all the world except in Israel" (2 Kings 5:15, NIV). Gehazi was serving a prophet and had seen firsthand the power of the God of Israel. Unfortunately, he decided to embrace the sin in his heart and left forever cursed because of it.

Discussion Questions

1. Are we willing to do what it takes to let God heal and restore us?

2. Are we humble enough to accept advice or a rebuke from those we think we're better than?

3. Are we willing to accept the future that God has for us even if it doesn't quite look like what we think it should?

→17←

Spiritual Warfare

We read in Ephesians 6:12 that,

Our struggle is not against flesh and blood, but against the rulers, against the authorities, against the powers of this dark world and against the spiritual forces of evil in the heavenly realms (NIV).

Think about that. People can be demon possessed or have demonic influences in their lives. We can take authority over those spirits in the name of Jesus, bind them, and cast them out. We can be filled with the Holy Spirit. The spiritual world is more real than the physical world. While the spiritual world can impact the physical world, the only way for us (as physical beings) to positively impact the spiritual world is through Jesus Christ. We must pray, aligning ourselves with God's will, plan, and purpose for our life.

And we are sure of this, that he will listen to us whenever we ask him for anything in line with his will. And if we really know he is listening when we talk to him and make our requests, then we can be sure that he will answer us (1 John 5:14-15, TLB).

The only way to defeat our spiritual enemies is through prayer. Satan understands the power of prayer more than we do because he's subjected to it *every day*!

Job 1 tells us that Job "was blameless and upright; he feared God and shunned evil" (Job 1:1, NIV). We're also told that he routinely sacrificed a burnt offering for each of his ten children to atone for their sins. The Bible says that Satan appeared before God, and God said, "Have you considered my servant Job? There is no one on earth like him; he is blameless and upright, a man who fears God and shuns evil." (Job 1:8, NIV) Satan said, "Job? Yeah, I've seen him. But, you're protecting him, his family, and everything he has, and I can't touch him!" That's the power of sacrifice and prayer!

The full weight, the full power, of who God is—is *always* with us, *always* available to us! We tend to only reach for Him during times of crisis or sickness. We sing songs declaring His power and victory over sin and death, but do we really believe it? We have to realize that *all* of who God is—is with us at all times.

Ephesians 6 details the armor of God—the belt of truth, the breastplate of righteousness, feet fitted with readiness that comes from the gospel, the shield of faith, the helmet of salvation, and the sword of the Spirit. Many a sermon has been preached on this subject, and I'm not going to regurgitate any of them. However, I understand it a little differently now than I have before.

In the military you're issued a helmet, flak jacket, load bearing vest, boots, etc. The only thing customized about those is that they're your size, and they will eventually smell like you. Each piece of the armor of God is custom fit to the wearer. Each piece is presented to that person as a precious gift, because it is. The helmet of salvation fits snug, but it's comfortable. It's not unwieldy; it doesn't feel heavy; it doesn't slow you down or limit your vision. The breastplate of righteousness fits perfectly. It doesn't restrict your breathing, it doesn't make your knees ache when you run, and it doesn't hinder you in battle. Each piece is custom designed and fitted just for you!

Talking about warfare and armor provides a different context for "taking thoughts captive." Second Corinthians 10:5 says,

We demolish arguments and every pretension that sets itself up against the knowledge of God, and we take captive every thought to make it obedient to Christ (NIV).

I've heard that verse since I was young and never really understood it. I always pictured it as being along the same lines as arresting someone. That person is stopped from doing something bad, but they're just gonna get out of jail and do it again. I viewed this as more of a delaying action rather than a cessation of activity.

People who are captured in war are supposed to be treated humanely in civilized society. They're supposed to have certain rights and aren't supposed to be tortured. But Satan doesn't believe in the Geneva Convention; he doesn't play fair. He hates us simply because we're created and loved by God. Let's look at a few realistic examples of what happens to captives. Women captured by ISIS are brutalized, and people have their heads cut off. The Mayans took captives for the sole purpose of sacrificing them. Other indigenous peoples were reported to take captives out of revenge for the sole purpose of torturing them.

Being a captive is not usually on anyone's bucket list. We're told to take captive all the thoughts that are not aligned with God's will, plan, and purpose for us. We don't treat them gently. We don't feed them; we starve them. We do away with them in Jesus' name because they're trying to lead us down the wrong path in order to kill us.

> *Temptation comes from the lure of our own evil desires. These evil desires lead to evil actions, and evil actions lead to death. So don't be misled my brothers and sisters. Whatever is good and perfect comes to us from God above...* (James 1:14-15, TLB).

Every thought, every desire, every action are stepping stones. We have to be aware of where they are leading us. Are these things leading us towards life or towards death?

First Peter 5:8 tells us that Satan "prowls around like a roaring lion looking for someone to devour" (NIV). I've watched enough *National Geographic* shows to know that lions deliberately stalk their prey. They frequently coordinate with other lions and slowly creep closer and closer. Then they spring into an attack, kill, and devour whatever it is. We're warned that Satan operates this same way. The truth is that he doesn't even have to kill us. If we're walking around scared, wounded, slowed down through guilt, shame, or whatever it may be, then we're less effective and can't complete what's been given to us to do.

It's so important to trust God completely and turn over to Him the areas of life that we've long controlled. We're taking something that we've maintained ownership of for a long time (maybe even most of our lives) and giving control of that to Jesus. It's important to understand and believe that He's going to meet that need better than we have. It's tough! Even so, we're much better off with Him in control than with us in control.

Discussion Questions

1. What is God asking you to turn over to Him?

2. What line(s) of thought do you need to take captive and eliminate in Jesus' name?

3. Has God shown you the direction some of your thoughts, desires, and actions are taking you?

✦18✦

Serving—Spiritual Gifts

We're often told that as we grow in Christ, we need to start reaching beyond ourselves and beyond the church we attend and we serve in. We're told that we need to reach the lost, and the passages for the Great Commission are dusted off and our memories refreshed. We're going through that season at my church, and I've been surprised at the opposition in my life when it comes to reaching out to share the gospel or even helping others.

There are things I've believed about myself for a long time that simply aren't true. These lies were designed to hold me back and to keep me from reaching out. I also understand enough about myself to know that my flesh will want me to help someone based on what I can get out of it. It sounds crazy to say, but I have to be careful because pride will try to guide me towards opportunities that feed it, and that's *not* where I want to be.

Take care! Don't do your good deeds publicly, to be admired, for then you will lose the reward from your Father in heaven. When you give a gift to a beggar, don't shout about it as the hypocrites do—blowing trumpets in the synagogues and streets to call attention to their acts of charity! I tell you in all earnestness, they have received all the reward they will ever get (Matthew 6:1-2, NLT).

Don't be selfish; don't live to make a good impression on others. Be humble, thinking of others as better than yourself. Don't just think about your own affairs, but be interested in others, too, and in what they are doing. Your attitude should be the kind that was shown us by Jesus Christ, who, though he was God, did not demand and cling to his rights as God, but laid aside his mighty power and glory, taking the disguise of a slave and becoming like men. And he humbled himself even further, going so far as actually to die a criminal's death on a cross (Philippians 2:3-8, NLT).

It's not like I needed further clarification that my sinful nature is wrong, but that's pretty clear. "Feed your pride and selfishness, and congratulations, you've failed." When we serve others, not only do we need to make sure our heart is properly aligned with Christ, we need to honor those we serve. If you look at Jesus' ministry, at no point did He belittle anyone nor was He ever condescending. He simply loved them and wanted them to be whole. He wanted them to have a loving relationship with the Father. We're to follow His example. To help us accomplish that, we've been empowered by the Holy Spirit to do certain things. Not just to do them, but to do them *well*.

Each of you should use whatever gift you have received to serve others, as faithful stewards of God's grace in its various forms. If anyone speaks, they should do so as one who speaks the very words of God. If anyone serves, they should do so with the strength God provides, so that in all things God may be praised through Jesus Christ (1 Peter 4:10-11, NIV).

God has given each of us the ability to do certain things well. So if God has given you the ability to prophesy, then prophesy whenever you can—as often as your faith is strong enough to receive a message from God. If your gift is that of serving others, serve them well. If you are a teacher, do a good job of teaching. If you are a preacher, see to it that your sermons are strong and helpful. If God has given you money, be generous in helping others with it. If God has given you administrative ability and put you in charge of the work of others, take the responsibility seriously (Romans 12:6-8, TLB).

Discovering our spiritual gifts isn't like taking a Myers-Briggs personality assessment or Gallup's StrengthsFinder assessment. It's about discovering our Kingdom purpose. Our physical abilities decline as we get older, but our spiritual gifts are just the opposite! The more we use them, the stronger they are, and the more attuned we are to the leading of the Holy Spirit. Our spiritual gifts are part of who we are, and they have to be refined and developed. We have to do the work and put in the repetitions in order to operate within our gifts naturally.

We've heard the saying, "Your life may be the only gospel someone ever reads." What we fail to understand is that *we* are ministers! Preaching the gospel isn't just done by the folks who stand behind the pulpit. Showing who Christ is on a day-in, day-out basis is *our* job! Do we hold ourselves to the same standards that we do pastors? Have we taken ownership of the gifts God has given us? Do we take our areas of ministry seriously? Do we prepare ourselves to share our testimony or lead someone to Christ? Do we preach to ourselves in order to move through (not past—through) whatever may be trying to take us down and choke us out?

In all that we do, we need to first ensure we're aligned with God's will and plan for our lives. If we're not, our efforts to serve others will amount to secular aid. We can do it by ourselves, but the outcome is completely different. It's God who brings the power and authority into our lives and blesses our efforts.

Paul summed it up well,

> *If I speak in the tongues of men or of angels, but do not have love, I am only a resounding gong or a clanging cymbal. If I have the gift of prophecy and can fathom all mysteries and all knowledge, and if I have a faith that can move mountains, but do not have love, I am nothing. If I give all I possess to the poor and give over my body to hardship that I may boast, but do not have love, I gain nothing* (1 Corinthians 13:1-3, NIV).

We can't give away something we don't own. It's so important to be connected to and pursuing Jesus. Who we are and what we do, need to come from a heart that's focused on God. Only then will our natural talents, abilities, and spiritual gifts mesh together smoothly and have an impact we never dreamed possible.

Discussion Questions

1. What is something God has put on your heart? Even if you feel it's a half-baked and far-out notion, what is it?

2. Are you praying that God will lead you into all that He's planned for you to do?

3. What is God saying to you right now?

⇥19⇤

John 6:26-28

In John 6, Jesus is teaching at a synagogue in Capernaum the day after feeding a crowd of 5,000 with five barley loaves and two fish. Those that He'd fed the day before were looking for Him and finally found Him on the other side of the lake, not knowing that He'd walked on water to meet the disciples the night before. Jesus plainly told them,

I can guarantee this truth: you're not looking for me because you saw miracles. You are looking for me because you ate as much of those loaves as you wanted. Don't work for food that spoils. Instead, work for the food that lasts into eternal life. This is the food the Son of Man will give you (John 6:26-27, GW).

As the discussion continues Jesus said,

I can guarantee this truth: Every believer has eternal life. I am the bread of life. Your ancestors ate the manna in the desert and died. This is the bread that comes from heaven so that whoever eats it won't die. I am the living bread that came from heaven. Whoever eats this bread will live forever. The bread I will give to bring life to the world is my flesh. ... If you don't eat the flesh of the Son of Man and drink his blood, you don't have the source of life in you. Those who eat my flesh and drink my blood have eternal life, and I will bring them back to life on the last day. My flesh is true food, and my blood is true drink. Those who eat my flesh and drink my blood live in me, and I live in them. The Father who has life sent me, and I live because of the Father. So those who feed on me will live because of me. This is the bread that came from heaven. It is not like the bread your ancestors ate. They eventually died. Those who eat this bread will live forever (John 6:47-51,53-58, GW).

The minds of Jesus' disciples were blown, along with everyone else in the crowd. He was talking about eating His flesh, drinking His blood, and living forever? What? Now, you have to understand—everyone there was hearing these words for the very first time. They didn't have the benefit of having 2,000+ years to study prophecies and compare them to what Jesus is saying. In the moment, they simply could not apply knowledge gained through events that had not yet occurred (such as the Last Supper, His crucifixion, and resurrection) in order to appreciate the fullness of what Jesus was saying to them. All they knew is that what He was saying was hard to comprehend. It just was not making sense.

In verses 61-63, Jesus turned to His disciples and said,

Does this offend you? Then what will you think if you see the Son of Man ascend to heaven again? The Spirit alone gives eternal life. Human effort accomplishes nothing. And the very words I have spoken to you are spirit and life (NLT).

At this point, many of Jesus' disciples left. He turned to the twelve and asks them, "Are you going to leave too?" I love Peter's response, "Lord, to whom would we go? You alone have the words that give eternal life" (John 6:66-68, The Book).

God's Word is full of hard things—some are hard to understand (parts of Ezekiel, Revelations), some are hard to read (Leviticus, Numbers), and some are hard to hear because it's truth. Jesus said,

For truly I tell you, until heaven and earth disappear, not the smallest letter, not the least stroke of a pen, will by any means disappear from the Law until everything is accomplished. Therefore anyone who sets aside one of the least of these commands and teaches others (to do likewise) will be called least in the kingdom of heaven, but whoever practices and teaches these commands will be called great in the kingdom of heaven (Matthew 5:18-19, NIV).

All of it applies. We don't get to pick and choose which parts we adhere to or follow. It's not a matter of convenience; it's a matter of obedience. I knew a guy that had been an infantryman in the Marine Corps and later did a ten-year stretch in prison. He said that being a Christian was *the* hardest thing he'd ever done. Why? Because we're called to surrender who we think we are, what we think we want and need, and follow Christ. We're to allow *Him* to define who we are, to provide what we need and to fulfill our desires. It's hard. But outside of Jesus Christ, true hope, love, forgiveness, life, freedom, and transformation simply do not exist. "Lord, to whom would we go? You alone have the words that give eternal life."

In Isaiah 55:8 God declares, "For my thoughts are not your thoughts, neither are your ways my ways" (NIV) I really like the way the New Living Translation puts it, "My thoughts are nothing like your thoughts ... and my ways are *far beyond* anything you could imagine" (emphasis mine).

We need to learn to think and act differently than we used to. Some aspects of the person we used to be can drop off immediately while other parts seem to never go away. Why? It's all part of the refining process that's designed to draw us to God. We must set ourselves aside, get out of our own way, and follow Jesus. We need to listen for His guidance. Listening involves being attentive and waiting—being ready to hear. When He speaks, we have to be prepared, to move if He says move or stay if He says stay.

Regardless of where you are in your walk with Christ, there will be hard words to hear and hard moments to go through. I think it's easy to sit in church or in a small group and proclaim, "God, I'll go wherever You want me to go! I'll do whatever it is You want me to do!" Then, once we're no longer in that setting, we revert back to what we know or what we've always done. I know I have. I'll get caught up in the moment and boldly declare something only to fall flat on my face almost as soon as I walk out of the building. I end up feeling like a failure and feel like I just can't do it.

Jesus told us that we can't do it on our own. Life is not easy, but Jesus will always be with us. When we are willing to listen and obey, then He is able to lead and guide us into all He has for us.

Discussion Questions

1. God's Word is full of hard teaching. What's one that is hard for you to hear and apply?

2. Some of what God tells us to do runs contrary to human logic. What's an example from your life of when God told you to do something that didn't make sense from the world's perspective?

3. What has the outcome of your obedience been so far?

→20←

Joshua 9-10

I want to look at Joshua's bold prayer in Joshua 10, where he asked God to make time stand still, from a slightly different angle. First, we have to backtrack a little bit.

In Deuteronomy 20, God gave Israel instructions for the conduct of war as they took over the Promised Land. He told them that it was okay to make peace with cities that were far away, but in verses 16-18 He says,

> *However, you must not spare anyone's life in the cities of these nations that the Lord your God is giving you as your property. You must claim the Hittites, Amorites, Canaanites, Perizzites, Hivites, and Jebusites for the Lord and **completely** destroy them, as the Lord your God has commanded you. Otherwise, they will teach you to do all the disgusting things they do for their gods, and you will sin against the Lord your God* (GW, emphasis mine).

The Message version says, "But with the towns of the people that God, **your** God, is giving you as an inheritance, it's different: don't leave anyone alive." Verse 18 gives us the why. "This is so there won't be any of them left to teach you to practice the abominations that they engage in with their gods and you end up sinning against God, *your* God." (emphasis mine) That's pretty straightforward, right? Not much to be confused about. Okay, now let's look at Joshua 9.

A large Hivite city in nearby Gibeon heard how the Israelites conquered Jericho and Ai. Even though the Hivites (also called Gibeonites because that's the city they lived in) had a reputation as being good fighters, they were afraid of Israel so they decided to try and trick Israel into making a peace treaty. They showed up wearing ratty clothes, worn out sandals, packing moldy bread and patched up wineskins, claiming to have come from far away.

Even though the Israelites were suspicious, they decided to hear the Gibeonites out. Verses 14 and 15 tell us,

> *So the Israelites examined their food, but they did not consult the Lord. Then Joshua made a peace treaty with them and guaranteed their safety, and the leaders of the community ratified their agreement with a binding oath* (NLT).

We know that all lies are eventually exposed, and this time was no different. Once the deception was realized, the Israelites were furious, but because of their oath, they didn't attack the city and kill everyone inside. Instead, Joshua cursed them and consigned them to be woodcutters and water carriers for the entire nation (verse 26).

As we move into Chapter 10, the Gibeonites came under attack by all the Amorite kings because of their alliance with Israel. Joshua marched all night to take the Amorites by surprise and along the way God told him, "Don't be afraid of them for I have given you victory over them." God caused the Amorites to panic and sent a massive hail storm that killed more of the enemy than Israel did, and ultimately God enabled Israel to conquer the Amorites.

Even though the Israelite leaders were suspicious of the Gibeonites, they didn't consult God as to what they should do. Instead, they chose to trust their own intellect and believed the Gibeonites' lies, making a peace treaty with them. I believe the Israelites' suspicion was the Holy Spirit advising them that the truth wasn't being presented. The end result is that these people, who were supposed to be completely destroyed because of their abominable acts and idolatry, were serving Israel by bringing wood and water to everyone on a daily basis. Even though they were servants, they were still interacting with the Israelite community on a daily basis. That one decision caused people, whom God said should be destroyed, to be woven into the fabric of Israel's society. Because of the pride of Israel's leaders, they were positioned right where God said they should not be. But God always shows up. Even when we're disobedient, even when we ignore the leading of the Holy Spirit, and even when we make bad decisions, God shows up and gives us victory.

There are things in each of our lives that God says don't belong there and should be removed and destroyed. Yet, we've made peace with whatever they are. In doing so, we have allowed the enemy to take up residence within us. We've opened the gate and allowed the enemy inside the wire. The very thing that wants to destroy you, now has permission to be there—and you've given it permission.

Discussion Questions

1. What have you given permission to be present in your life that doesn't belong?

2. What has God told you to be done with, to destroy, to remove completely, but you're still holding onto?

3. Why are you not trusting God with that area of your life?

→21←

It Is Well With My Soul

"It is well with my soul." Man, that's such a deep place of contentment. To be able to truthfully say that in the midst of any circumstance would be amazing, wouldn't it? Kristine DiMarco, one of the worship leaders at Bethel Church wrote a song titled, "It is Well" and said in an interview that she wrote it because, "My faith is *faith* and is not just hope. We can hope God is real our whole lives, but why not *know* that He is real?" (emphasis mine)

I've been in very difficult circumstances in life, and at the time, I just wanted to know that there was hope, that I wouldn't be stuck there forever, and that someone else had gone through this same thing and not only survived but was living on the other side of it. Hope is *very* powerful. It's been credited with keeping prisoners of war alive. It's kept people going when all they wanted to do was lay down and die. Having hope that you'll survive is different than having faith in the one rescuing you.

Jesus talks about faith and says,

The Kingdom of Heaven is like a mustard seed planted in a field. It is the smallest of all seeds, but it becomes the largest of garden plants; it grows into a tree, and birds come and make nests in its branches (Matthew 13:31-32, NLT).

Now, mustard seeds are between 1-2mm in diameter. BBs are 4.5mm, so in comparison, mustard seeds are, at a minimum, less than half that size. The mustard plant generally grows 6-8 feet tall, although it's not uncommon for the plants to reach 10 feet in height, and they can be just as wide as they are tall. It's so interesting that Jesus compares the kingdom of heaven to a large plant that grows from such a small seed and provides safety, shelter, and rest to those who find it.

Jesus knew that a life of hope was one of survival, but a life of faith was one of relationship. Everything He said and did was in lockstep with God the Father.

I tell you the truth, the Son can do nothing by himself. He does only what he sees the Father doing. Whatever the Father does, the Son also does (John 5:19, NLT).

I don't speak on my own authority. The Father who sent me has commanded me what to say and how to say it (John 12:49, NLT).

The Bible tells us that Jesus often went off by Himself to pray and seek God. He did this to stay connected, or in tune, with God. He wanted to make sure that everything about Him brought glory to the Father. He wanted to accomplish the things He had been sent here to do. Jesus never knew a moment without God's presence in His life until right before His death on the cross when God had to look away because all the sins of the world came crashing down on Jesus.

We've all been in big trouble as kids. There may even have been a time when you're suddenly called into the boss' office to explain something and have felt the dread that comes along with that. Can you imagine the weight Jesus bore as the sins of the entire world were laid on Him? We talk about how He paid the price for our sins, but have we ever considered the enormity of it? He became the sacrifice, making atonement for every sin committed by every person for all of time. The sins of Hitler, Stalin, Pol Pot, the people committing genocide in Africa, Charles Manson, Jeffrey Dahmer, serial rapists, child pornographers, you, and me were all laid on Him as though He had committed them.

Jesus said,

If anyone wants to be a follower of mine, let him deny himself and take up his cross and follow me. For anyone who keeps his life for himself shall lose it; and anyone who loses his life for me shall find it again (Matthew 16:24-25, TLB).

I reached a point in life where I didn't just hope that Jesus could set me free, I *knew* He was the only one who could. I had hope that my situation would improve, but again, I had faith (I knew) that ceasing to be whom I used to be ("let him deny himself and take up his cross") and following Jesus would be the *only* way that was going to happen.

Jesus came to earth as a man and lived a blameless life before God. He suffered everything we do—the emotions, the temptations, etc.—yet he did not sin. Think about His life and imagine all that He went through. I have no doubt that His flesh wanted to rise up at different times. The Bible tells us that He didn't necessarily want to go to the cross, *but* He chose obedience over desire. He chose His relationship with the Father over what His flesh wanted. Jesus had faith (He *knew*) that the Father's plan was perfect. Jesus knew that what He was doing would accomplish the Father's will and make an eternal difference.

We've been promised that on judgment day, God will end Satan's reign.

You will be brought down to the pit of hell, down to its lowest depths. Everyone there will stare at you and ask, "Can this be the one who shook the earth and the kingdoms of the world? Can this be the one who destroyed the world and made it into a shambles, who demolished its greatest cities and had no mercy on his prisoners? (Isaiah 14:15-17, TLB)

On our own, we're no match for Satan. We're just not. However, we're not alone. We have the full power, might, and majesty of *the* Creator living inside of us. We have to stop trying to fix ourselves and rely on Jesus to guide us away from the things we used to do and into a deep relationship with Him. Jesus didn't suffer and die so we could limp along in survival mode. He died so that we can accomplish amazing things in His Kingdom! He has a specific plan and purpose for your life. We need to stay connected to Him in order to achieve all that God has for us to do.

Discussion Questions

1. What could you accomplish if you lived a life of faith where you trusted God in every area and with everything?

2. In what area of your life do you need to develop more faith?

3. What does it look like when you choose obedience to God over your desires?

→22←

Revelation 12:10-11

It has happened at last—the salvation and power and kingdom of our God, and the authority of his Christ! For the Accuser has been thrown down to earth—the one who accused our brothers and sisters before our God day and night. And they defeated him because of the blood of the Lamb and because of their testimony (Revelations 12:10-11, The Book).

When I read the part where it says we will be victorious "because of the blood of the Lamb," it made sense to me. Jesus paid the price for our sins, once and for all. Because of Him, we've been redeemed and set free. But the part of that verse that piqued my interest is where it says we'll be victorious in part "because of their testimony."

The word "testimony" as used here comes from the Greek word *martyria* (mar-too-ree'-ah) which means evidence given, reputation, witness, record, report."[1] We take part in defeating Satan because there's evidence given concerning our reputation, our character, and the things we've done. Think about that for a minute—our obedience to God isn't just about being a better Christian. Obedience is not a wimpy or cowering act done in fear. It's the complete opposite! When we're obedient, we're *actively* choosing God over Satan. Our choices, our lives, matter more than we realize. *Who* we are matters!

Jesus said, "Humans can reproduce only human life, but the Holy Spirit gives new life from heaven" (John 3:6, TLB).

There must be a spiritual renewal of your thoughts and attitudes. You must display a new nature because you are a new person, created in God's likeness—righteous, holy, and true (Ephesians 4:23-24, The Book)

Who you are inside eventually shows up on the outside. As we walk out our salvation, change happens internally first and is later made manifest externally. I know I felt different long before I *acted* differently. We have to stop looking for a reason to give in to the broken areas of our lives and instead, look for a reason to win.

> *Beware of false prophets. They come to you disguised as sheep, but in their hearts they are vicious wolves. You will know them by what they produce. People don't pick grapes from thorn bushes or figs from thistles, do they? In the same way every good tree produces good fruit, but a rotten tree produces bad fruit. A good tree cannot produce bad fruit, and a rotten tree cannot produce good fruit. Any tree that fails to produce good fruit is cut down and thrown into a fire. So you will know them by what they produce* (Matthew 7:15-20, GW).

Our lives produce fruit by which we are known. This fruit is what defines our character which builds our reputation. Jesus talked about this in His own life.

> *If you trust me, you are really trusting God who sent me. For when you see me, you are seeing the one who sent me. …all who reject me and my message will be judged at the day of judgment by the truth I have spoken. I don't speak on my own authority. The Father who sent me gave me his own instructions as to what I should say. And I know his instructions lead to eternal life; so I say whatever the Father tells me to say!* (John 12:44-45, 48-50, The Book).

Jesus wanted to make sure people knew and understood that everything He said, everything He did, and everything about Him was directly from His Father. That's such a humble place to operate from! Here He is, *the* Son of God, and He's making sure that all the credit and all the honor, goes to God the Father.

I like watching rugby from time to time. It has all the pace of soccer and the physicality of the NFL without all of the commercials. At the end of a match, you can tell who played and who didn't. The guys who played are sweaty and bloody; their face is swollen in places; their uniform is dirty and ripped. The guys who didn't play are clean and most likely don't smell as bad. They're still big, physical guys to be sure, but they just don't look as imposing as the guys who played.

I also like reading books and watching movies or documentaries about the Special Operations guys. Each man believes that there's nothing he can't accomplish, and no obstacle he can't overcome. They firmly believe and have faith in their training. Put that man with his brothers-in-arms and together, there's very little they can't do, no adversary they cannot destroy, and no objective they cannot accomplish. I find a lot of similarity between their mentality and the reality of our spiritual life.

Satan will try every tactic to delay us and separate us from our brothers and our families. He will destroy us if given a chance. We have to meet every attack with a higher level of intensity, be more committed, and be more willing to do what it takes. We have to look for a way to win. I want to appear before God on judgment day battered, bruised, and bloodied from battle. I want to stand there victorious. That's not going to just happen on its own, though. It takes effort. It takes commitment. It takes sacrifice.

Paul advises us to

Let heaven fill your thoughts. Do not think only about things down here on earth. For you died when Christ died, and your real life is hidden with Christ in God (Colossians 3:2-3, The Book).

Jesus promises that,

Everyone who is victorious shall eat of the hidden manna, the secret nourishment from heaven; and I will give to each a white stone, and on the stone will be engraved a new name that no one else knows except the one receiving it (Revelations 2:17, TLB).

God knows the person He created us to be and all the things we're capable of doing. Only by pressing into Him will we be able to become the man we're supposed to be. Only by becoming the person we are designed, created, and purposed to be will we ever be able to stand victorious before Him. Adversity is guaranteed. Our reaction and response, in the face of it, is what defines who we are. Through the power of Jesus' name, we're not just enabled to defeat Satan—we're guaranteed to do so.

Discussion Questions

1. What does it mean to you to "Look for a way to win?"
2. Do you see yourself as having a lead role, as being a pivotal force, in kingdom battles?
3. Are you walking through this life as though you have an active role in God's plan?

[1] Strong's Concordance, Greek—3141

⇥23⇤

God Has Been Faithful to Me

Earlier this week I was watching a video of a Christian song-writer talking about the events and thoughts behind one of their songs. In the course of relating the story, the songwriter said that as they considered everything that had gone on in their life, they realized that God had been so faithful to them. I recently heard a sermon where the preacher talked about how God is faithful to us. What stands out to me in both of these instances is how I perceived the concept of God being faithful to us. In my mind, faithfulness applies to human relationships.

We're faithful to our spouse, to a friend in need, and so on. A dog can be faithful to its master. The thought of God being faithful to me aggravated me for some reason, which didn't make sense. So, I started looking at scriptures and at myself. This is what I understand so far.

In Exodus 3, God appeared to Moses in a burning bush and told him to lead the Israelites out of Egypt. Moses protested and in verse 13 asked God, "If I go to the people of Israel and tell them, "The God of your ancestors has sent me to you," they will ask me, "What is his name?" Then what should I tell them?" God replied, "I AM WHO I AM" (NLT).

> In the beginning you laid the foundations of the earth, and the heavens are the work of your hands. They will perish, but you remain; they will all wear out like a garment. Like clothing you will change them and they will be discarded. But you remain the same, and your years will never end (Psalm 102:25-27, NIV).

"I am the Lord," he says, "and there is no other. I publicly pro-claim bold promises. I do not whisper obscurities in some dark corner so no one can understand what I mean. And I did not tell the people of Israel to ask me for something I did not plan to give" (Isaiah 45:18-19, NLT).

I am the Lord, and I do not change (Malachi 3:6, NLT).

Don't misunderstand why I have come. I did not come to abolish the law of Moses or the writings of the prophets. No, I came to accomplish their purpose. I tell you the truth, until heaven and earth disappear, not even the smallest detail of God's law will disappear until its purpose is achieved (Matthew 5:17-18, NLT).

I am the Alpha and the Omega, the Beginning and the End, says the Lord God, He Who is and Who was and Who is to come, the Almighty (the Ruler of all) (Revelations 1:8, AMP).

God *is*. There's no deviation of His character or His nature, never has been, never will be. So, why did those references to His faithfulness to us irk me? I didn't understand why, and as I prayed about what I was thinking and feeling, God showed me other things that frustrate me. You know, because that's exactly the answer I was hoping for.

As I read through the Old Testament, it always stands out to me that the Israelites had to wander through the desert for 40 years because of their unbelief and disobedience. Once they finally crossed the Jordan River and took possession of the Promised Land, they began to stray from God and started worshipping idols. They abandoned His ways, ignored the prophets He sent, and ended up being conquered and taken out of the land God promised them because of their sins.

When I read all of this, I shook my head and thought, *Man—why didn't you all get this? God Himself has been leading, guiding, pro-tecting, and instructing you. Now, He's warning you that what you're doing is wrong and telling you in pretty plain terms what's going to happen, and you're just going to ignore all that? What is wrong with you?! Why can't you just leave all that nonsense behind?*

I get frustrated with the Israelites in the Old Testament, but if I take an honest look at my own life, I'm no better. God tells me to do stuff, and I basically ignore Him because it's hard or because it seems too random. It's disobedience, plain and simple. I get frustrated because I'm figuratively circling the desert just like the Israelites, and I don't want to be there. I get very annoyed with this aspect of my life.

I had a conversation with a guy who's been a Christian longer than I've been alive. (That didn't used to mean very much, but it's starting to!) He told me that the older he gets, the harder things become physically, mentally, emotionally, and morally. That last one jolted me! I wasn't able to ask about it at the time, but I've thought about it a lot since. What I'm coming to understand is that each one of us has a root of brokenness within us.

In Romans 7, the Apostle Paul talks about wanting to do what is right but instead does the very things he hates. Paul had his root of brokenness; I've got mine; you've got yours. That root is *the* main strike against the person we're supposed to be. But as we continue down the path of righteousness, we're continually being refined. The farther you go with Jesus Christ, the more refining you go through. The easy stuff comes off first, then bigger stuff, then bigger still, until (hopefully) we're left with just that root of brokenness. The truth is that we can't kill it on our own. We can't fix it or make it go away. At some point we have to acknowledge this, turn to God, and seek Him in a deeper way.

In Mark 4:35-41, we're told the story of Jesus rebuking a storm that threatened to sink the boat He and the disciples were on. Just as the wind and waves obeyed His command to be still then, He speaks peace and calm into whatever situation we're facing today. God is everlasting to everlasting. He is true. He is just, righteous, and faithful to His Word. The storms in our life know His name and obey His commands. We have to remember that our enemies know the power of prayer better than we do because they are subjected to it *every day*. They know the power of Jesus' name in no uncertain terms. *They* know He is faithful and just. *They* know we're created in His image and that we're His sons. Do we?

God's character is well known; it's been documented for thousands of years by numerous people, and it is unchanging. My faithfulness to Him is what's in question. Sometimes we want to blame someone else instead of accepting responsibility for our conduct and actions. We can shirk what's ours to do, try to lay that responsibility at someone else's feet, or we can do something about it. Which one will we choose?

My problems, irritations, and annoyances have nothing to do with God being faithful to us. They have to do with me. I need to be faithful to *Him*. We need to ask God to show us the broken areas of our life and ask Him to heal them. We need to stop circling around or avoiding these issues in our lives and purposely engage them. We need to strike at our root of brokenness in Jesus' name. It's time to stop being comfortable where we are. It's time to break cover and bring the fight to the enemy.

We've all seen TV shows or movies where the bad guys are barricaded in a building with hostages, and the hero turns to his partner and says, "I'm goin' in—cover me." At that point they pop up, crank off a few shots, and run towards their adversary. While they're rushing forward, everyone else lets loose with a barrage of bullets that pins the enemy down so their comrade can safely advance.

That's what we can do for each other spiritually. When we start going after what God puts on our heart or what He's showing us we need to do, we need to look to our wives, the man on our right and on our left, and tell them, "I'm goin' in—cover me." Our prayers pin down and destroy the enemy so that our wife, our kids, and our brothers and sisters in Christ can move forward into what God has for them. We all have things we struggle with, but do we have someone we're accountable to who lifts us up in prayer? We have to be deliberate to build that into our lives.

Some guys know me better than I'm comfortable with. But it's not about my comfort—it's about pushing through whatever that obstacle is. It's about becoming the person I'm supposed to be. Dr. Martin Luther King Jr once said, "Change does not roll in on wheels of inevitability but comes through continuous struggle." This is a fight.

Discussion Questions

1. Do we live like we're in a battle?

2. Do you have a brother in Christ that you're accountable to? If not, why?

3. What issue(s) are causing you to circle around in the desert like the Israelites because of your disobedience?

→24←

Disciples

A husband and wife were talking about their different parenting styles, and the husband said, "The more I seek God and the more (my wife) seeks God, the more our hearts, choices, and parenting styles reflect His ways." I thought that was awesome! They find common ground through seeking God, not through compromise. Neither of them loses to the other, but because they are both committed to seeking and pleasing God, He brings them together. As I thought about all the ways we should keep our focus on God and the fact that we're His disciples, I was reminded of Proverbs 3:6. It tells us, "In all thy ways acknowledge Him, and He shall direct thy paths" (KJV).

These commandments that I give you today are to be on your hearts. Impress them on your children. Talk about them when you sit at home and when you walk along the road, when you lie down and when you get up. Tie them as symbols on your hands and bind them on your foreheads. Write them on the doorframes of your houses and on your gates (Deuteronomy 6:6-9, NIV)

We are to keep His commands and standards before us at all times. They should define our lifestyle, not just be part of our lives. This unwavering, unrelenting focus brings about transformation.

In Luke 6 we're told that Jesus prayed all night, then selected twelve men out of the crowd that was following Him to be His disciples. To be one of Jesus' chosen disciples was to be part of an elite group. It still is. Webster's dictionary defines a disciple as, "one who accepts and assists in spreading the doctrines of another." That's nice, but it is not exactly the model given us by the original twelve who were chosen by Jesus. These men gave up their jobs, their families, their homes. They gave up *everything* to follow Jesus. Their lives were *consumed* by Him. They were in a day-in, day-out relationship with Jesus Christ. They followed Him and listened to His teachings; they watched what He did and how He did it.

For His part, Jesus kept everyone's focus on the Father by healing people in different ways instead of teaching phrases and methods that would've ended up as powerless rote phrases and practices. He taught the masses in parables but explained them to His disciples. In this setting, a disciple is a learner or a follower—someone learning from a master. In his book *Growing True Disciples*, George Barna points out that "Discipleship is not a program. It is not a ministry. It is a life-long commitment to a lifestyle."[1] A little later in the book he says, "Discipleship is a life-long calling that demands every resource we will ever muster. Discipleship is about a passion to reach our full potential in Jesus Christ."[2] We're not in training to become youth pastors, missionaries, or any other vocation. We're called to follow Him.

> *For the word of God is full of living power. It is sharper than the sharpest knife, cutting deep into our innermost thoughts and desires. It exposes us for what we really are. Nothing in all creation can hide from him. Everything is naked and exposed before his eyes. This is the God to whom we must explain all that we have done* (Hebrews 4:12-13, The Book, emphasis mine).

We need to be honest with ourselves regarding where we're at in our spiritual journey. As I examine myself, it seems that no matter what I do, it's just never enough. But that's just it—it never will be. We're not called to *do* for Jesus Christ; we're called to *be* His disciples. It's through our relationship with Jesus that He's able to refine us, lead us forward.

The Apostle Paul said,

It's not that I've already reached the goal or have already com-
*pleted the course. But **I run to win that which Jesus Christ has***
***already won for me.** Brothers and sisters, I can't consider myself*
a winner yet. This is what I do: I don't look back, I lengthen my
stride, and I run straight toward the goal to win the prize that
God's heavenly call offers in Christ Jesus (Philippians 3:12-14,
GW, emphasis mine).

Jesus tells us, "Anyone who puts a hand to the plow and then
looks back is not fit for the Kingdom of God" (Luke 9:62, NLT).

In 1519 Hernan Cortes landed in South America with 500
soldiers and a serious desire for gold. As they started to push in-
land, he ordered that the ships be burned. Why? This left his men
with exactly two choices: succeed or die. There was no other way
out. Our choices today aren't that dissimilar.

Jesus tells us that, "No one can serve two masters" (Matthew
6:24, GW). For me, it boils down pretty plainly. We can follow
Jesus Christ, or we can go back to being the pile of garbage we
were before *He* set us free. *He* has given us a new life, a new identity, and a position within *His* Kingdom. If we truly are Christ-followers, then our thoughts, choices, and actions will reflect that
reality.

Are we living our lives in such a way that we reflect who He is?
I'm not talking about the "pastel Jesus" in pictures showing a
skinny guy holding a lamb and looking serene. I mean Jesus of
Nazareth—an old school carpenter. He was a manly man, a man
who spoke with such authority that people were drawn to Him. He
was someone who, even though he was tired, hungry, and thirsty,
seized the opportunity to minister to a Samaritan woman who
needed restoration. He had zero tolerance for the superficial acts of
religion being demonstrated by the Pharisees. He demonstrated ultimate submission to our heavenly Father in the Garden of
Gethsemane. This is the God to whom we will answer for how
we've lived our lives.

Discussion Questions

1. Paul talks about "lengthening his stride," stretching out even as he continues his lifelong race. What area of life are you lengthening your stride in?

2. How do your thoughts, choices, and actions reflect that you are a Christ-follower?

3. What are the things in your life that need destroyed or torn down with God's help to ensure you focus on moving forward with Christ?

[1] George Barna, Growing True Disciples, (Colorado, Waterbrook, 2001), p19.
[2] Ibid., p99.

⇒25⇐

Independence Day

A husband and wife are strolling along a shaded path that meanders through a park, holding hands, laughing, and talking about the future. Suddenly, the wife tears her hand from her husband's grasp and rushes over to a homeless man that's standing 30-40 feet off of the path. She embraces him tightly, takes his hands, gazes longingly into his eyes, and kisses him passionately. The wife whispers how much she's missed him and, with a backward glance, begins walking back towards her husband. Her face still flush with excitement, she somewhat sheepishly explains, "I'm sorry, honey. I know we have a great life together, and you're absolutely everything I've ever wanted in a husband. But I've known that man for a long time, and every time I see him I just can't help myself."

Don't we do the same thing when we walk away from God and embrace sin? Yes, there are temptations, pitfalls, and trials in life, and we're not always going to win that battle. But are we deliberately choosing to disengage from the One who knows us best and loves us most in favor of someone who has nothing of value to offer and wants to destroy us? We need to stay connected to Jesus Christ who did *everything* possible to enable us to have a relationship with Him. He sets us free and then allows us to choose whether or not we will serve Him. That, in itself, is amazing to me. We don't have to pick Him, but why wouldn't we?

Since you were brought back to life with Christ, focus on the things that are above—where Christ holds the highest position. Keep your mind on things above, not on worldly things. You have died, and your life is hidden with Christ in God. Christ is your life. When he appears, then you, too, will appear with him in glory. Therefore, put to death whatever is worldly in you: your sexual sin, perversion, passion, lust, and greed (which is the same thing as worshiping wealth). It is because of these sins that God's anger comes on those who refuse to obey him. You used to live that kind of sinful life. Also get rid of your anger, hot tempers, hatred, cursing, obscene language, and all similar sins. Don't lie to each other. you've gotten rid of the person you used to be and the life you used to live, and you've become a new person. This new person is continually renewed in knowledge to be like its Creator. Where this happens, there is no Greek or Jew, circumcised or uncircumcised, barbarian, uncivilized person, slave, or free person. Instead, Christ is everything and in everything (Colossians 3:1-11, GW).

I love that passage! "You used to live that kind of sinful life" (but) "you've become a new person."

On July 4th of every year, we celebrate our nation's Independence Day and take the time to recognize all that is great about our country. But each one of us has our own Independence Day. We each have a story of how we were set free from the bonds that held us in servitude to a cruel master that hates us. We need to never forget that day either. And while we should never forget who we were, and thus risk becoming self-righteous, the goal is not to stay captive to the memory of the person we used to be but to continue forward in Jesus Christ.

I'm reminded of the lyrics from the old hymn "I Have Decided to Follow Jesus": "The cross before me, the world behind me. No turning back. No turning back." We all have a past, but that is not our focus. Just as we don't drive around looking only in the rearview mirror, we cannot remain focused on the person we used to be. We must take ownership of who Jesus says we are. We must accept how He sees us and let go of the person we became on our own. We have been set free to become the one God designed, created, and purposed us to be. *That* is the personal reality we must own. We must embrace all of who Christ is and stay focused on our relationship with Him.

Discussion Questions

1   As you walk through this life with Jesus, there are times when you let go of His hand in order to pursue something else. What is it?

2. What lies about yourself are you still believing (I'm an angry guy, I always…)?

3. What truth about you is Christ wanting you to embrace?

✣26✣

David, Solomon, Rehoboam

I frequently think about David, Solomon, and Rehoboam. David had a strong relationship with God and a deep love for Him so much so that God declared him "a man after my own heart" (Acts 13:22, NLT). If you go back and read through 1 Chronicles 28 and 29, you'll see who he is at the end of his life and the things that matter to him.

For most of his life, David wanted to build a temple to honor God. He carefully drew up the plans and obsessed over every detail for decades. However, God told David that he was not to be the one to build the temple. In a very solemn moment, David passed the plans to build the Temple, the drawings for the courtyards, the division of priestly duties, and the material lists to do all of these things to his son Solomon. In addition, David donated his private treasure of 112 tons of gold and 262 tons of refined silver to be used for building the Temple, then challenged the leaders of Israel to follow his example. David led the nation in a prayer of praise to the Lord, and then, having been king over all of Israel for 40 years, he passed the crown to Solomon.

One of the first things Solomon did was to take all the leaders of the nation out to the tabernacle and offer burnt offerings to God. Second Chronicles 1:7 tells us that,

God appeared to Solomon in a dream and said, "What do you want? Ask, and I will give it to you!" (The Book)

Of all the things that Solomon could have asked for, his request was

Give me wisdom and knowledge that I may lead this people, for

who is able to govern this great people of yours? (2 Chronicles 1:10, NIV)

God heard his heart and granted him not only wisdom and knowledge but also promises to give him "riches, wealth, and honor such as no other king has ever had before you or will ever have again!" (v.12, The Book)

Fast forward to the end of Solomon's life as described in 1 Kings 11, and we see that Solomon allowed himself to be led away from God and began worshiping idols. Verse 6 tells us that, "

Solomon did what was evil in the Lord's sight; he refused to follow the Lord completely, as his father, David, had done (The Book).

Because of his willful disobedience, God grew angry with Solomon, and the rest of his life is spent dealing with rebels. Solomon reigned over all of Israel for 40 years.

Solomon's son, Rehoboam, became the next king. He was king over all of Israel for a whole three days before his pride and arrogance caused the nation to split. In 1 Kings, a whopping 34 verses of scripture summarize Rehoboam's reign, and none of it was impressive. Rehoboam was the king of Judah for 17 years.

David passed on a strong legacy to Solomon. Not just politically or economically, but more importantly *spiritually*. Solomon started out strong but allowed himself to be pulled off course by his own willfulness and pride. He finished his days knowing that God was going to tear the kingdom apart because of *his* disobedience. One of the things that strikes me in all of this is that when God confronted David with his sin, he repented and was on his face. When God warned Solomon about his idolatry and sin, he didn't repent. He just kept going down the path he was on. The legacy that Rehoboam inherited was a kingdom that had peaked and was now crumbling. He had no strength of character and no desire to lead well. More importantly, he had no relationship with God.

Life can be equated to a relay race where one generation passes the baton to the next. Each one of us has been passed the baton in one form or another. Some of us were handed a baton that was too heavy, and we could barely carry it. Some of us were handed a baton that left us with wounds that never quite seemed to heal. Some of us were handed a baton that was too light, and when the pressures and trials of life came about, we struggled to maintain our proper course.

It's not always fair or deserved, but the condition of the baton we receive isn't something we can control or have a choice in. What we do with it *is* our responsibility. So, how do we position those in our life like David positioned Solomon? Is it simply a matter of going to church? Praying at meal times? Not cursing too much or not watching porn when the kids are around? What condition will the baton be in when we pass it on? Will it be better than what we received?

One place where I was stationed when I was in the military had a mirror that was mounted on a side wall right before you walked out the front doors. We always took the opportunity to check ourselves over before going out to make sure we were squared away. At the top of the mirror was a challenge that had been taped there probably eons beforehand, and you'd see it every time you looked in the mirror. It read, "If you were accused of being a Marine, would there be enough evidence to convict you?"

So it is with us today. When we're judged before the throne of God, will He say to us, "Well done good and faithful servant!"? Will we be declared to be a man after God's own heart? Will we hear those words? David told Solomon,

> *Observe what the Lord your God requires: Walk in obedience to him and keep his decrees and commands, his laws and regulations, as written in the Law of Moses. Do this so that you may prosper in all you do and wherever you go...* (1 Kings 2:3, NIV).

Do what God's word says. Don't merely listen to it, or you will fool yourselves (James 1:22, GW).

As Christians, we tend to focus on what we're doing. We've talked before about how God's not primarily looking for our acts of service—He's looking for us to give more of ourselves to Him. But action is involved in that process. There are things that are ours to do, but we should not endeavor to do them without Him. We have to be intentional in our pursuit of Jesus and allow him to refine and purify us.

Discussion Questions

1. Are you allowing God more access to who you are?

2. Are you asking Him to show you the things in your heart and mind that aren't pleasing to Him? What are you doing about it once He does?

3. What condition will the baton be in when you hand it off (what kind of legacy are you creating)?

→27←

The Battle Within

*The old sinful nature loves to do evil, which is just opposite from what the Holy Spirit wants. And the Spirit gives us desires that are opposite from what the sinful nature desires. These two forces are constantly fighting each other, and your choices are **never** free from this conflict* (Galatians 5:17, NLT, emphasis mine)

In his book, *From the Pinnacle of the Temple*, Dr Charles Farah says,

> There may be a lull in the battle, but there's never a cessation of hostilities. There is no simple solution (or spiritual formula) that will solve all our problems. We may as well face the harsh fact that the war will never be over... until we reach the other side.[1]

That's the reality of where we are. Our real struggle is within, and it is between the person we used to be and the one we're supposed to be. I'm sick and tired of having the old me around. No, I'm not the person I used to be by a long shot, but in no way shape or form have I arrived. I previously shared the story of a note on a mirror at one of my old workplaces that offered a challenge. Putting that challenge in the context of our spiritual walk, it would read, "If you were accused of being a Christ-follower, would there be enough evidence to convict you?"

I've had that opportunity the last couple weeks and found myself lacking. If I measure myself against God's righteousness, His grace, His love, His hatred of sin, I simply don't make the grade. I know we can't meet His standards on our own, but I get frustrated and angry that I'm not more than what I am. I'm on the path of righteousness, I'm pressing forward, but when I look at what is not fully submitted, I'm not at all okay with it.

Unless you are faithful in small matters, you won't be faithful in large ones. If you cheat even a little, you won't be honest with greater responsibilities (Luke 16:10, NLT).

Faithfulness requires us to step out and do what we know He has for us to do. This process will cost us who we think we are and will change the focus of our lives. But the goal is not to arrive safely at death. The goal is to stop being who we were and start being the person we were designed, created, and purposed to be! We cannot shy away from the hard work of pushing aside the false image of ourselves and grasping the vision of who God says we are! Anything less ain't gonna get it done.

You have tested us, O God; you have purified us like silver melted in a crucible. You captured us in your net and laid the burden of slavery on our backs. You sent troops to ride across our broken bodies. We went through fire and flood. But you brought us to a place of great abundance (Psalm 66:10-12, NLT).

The Apostle Paul says,

For I have learned to be content whatever the circumstances. I know what it is to be in need, and I know what it is to have plenty. I have learned the secret of being content in any and every situation, whether well fed or hungry, whether living in plenty or in want. I can do all this through him who gives me strength (Philippians 4:11-13, NLT).

Are we grateful for the trials and tribulations? Are we taking stock of ourselves each time we encounter something within that doesn't measure up or simply doesn't belong?

In one job I had, we performed major maintenance actions that affected every single aspect of our facility. At the end of it, we'd get the guys together and go over the entire event to hash out what worked well and what didn't. We'd discuss it all and document it for the next time. In a relatively short time period, we mastered a complex event and found that we were able to do even more in the same amount of time. Do we take this approach in our spiritual life? Do we take a look at the last time we blew it and step through that event with God? Do we ask Him to show us our heart and how we can do it better or differently the next time? Do we engage our wife or a trusted friend in open (and loving) conversation about what they see going on in us?

I've had the privilege of having my wife engage me about things she's been seeing that don't belong. I don't mind telling you that it was tough. It hurt. I was offended and upset with her at first, and it took me the better part of a day to get past it. But, she was obedient to God and called out the truth in love. I hated to hear where I wasn't, but I needed to hear it. "Remember, it is sin to know what you ought to do and then not do it" (James 4:17, NLT).

Once we hear from God, we have the responsibility to do something about it. We don't have the luxury of ignorance. We've been told, now we know, and we're responsible. Being a Christ-follower isn't mindless obedience. It's the deliberate choice to follow the will and plans of the Creator. It doesn't matter whether we want to, whether we agree with it in that moment, whether we understand the "why" behind His direction, or not. God is looking for men that will accept Him as Lord of their lives, that will seek His face, and that will follow Him no matter what.

Discussion Questions

1. Are you choosing God's way over your desires?
2. What refining process is God walking you through now?
3. What heart change is being brought about through this?

1. Charles Farah, From the Pinnacle of the Temple, (New Jersey, Bridge Logos Foundation, 1979), p59.

⊹28⊹

Hearts Coming Alive

I love the Lord because he hears and answers my prayers. Because he bends down and listens, I will pray as long as I have breath! (Psalm 116:1-2, The Book)

Every time I read through Psalm 116, that passage stands out to me. The psalmist loves the Lord because He listens and answers. I remember when my wife and I started dating. We would hang out and talk for hours! It felt good just to be around her. We didn't have to be talking or doing anything special; I just wanted to be around her. When I wasn't with her, I was thinking about her. Even now, I'm looking forward to retirement so I can spend more time with her. Hopefully, she feels the same way. ;-)

As I was thinking about how things were when I was courting my wife, God asked me, "What do you love about me?" The first thing that came to my mind was, "Because You love me." Right behind that thought was, "Because You use people like me." I cannot tell you how powerful that is! I know who I was before Jesus Christ pulled me out of the tar pit I was stuck in. The thing I'm most grateful for is that not only did He rescue me and call His own, God led me away from the person I used to be. He has lovingly been showing me who I am in Him, refining and purifying me as we walk along the path of righteousness together.

God doesn't shy away from spending time with imperfect people. He loves us and cares about us—who we are and how we are all matter to Him. Jesus wants a close relationship with us. He wants to heal and restore us. He demonstrated that during His physical ministry here on earth and, if my life is an indicator, He's still doing it today.

Mark 5:25-29 tells the story of a woman who had been suffering for twelve years. She spent all of her money on doctors and was now not only poor, but her condition was worse. She heard about all that Jesus had done and thought to herself, "If only I could touch his clothes, I know I will be healed" (v.28, TPT). This poor woman had suffered for so long! She wanted and needed her suffering to end and knew that Jesus was her last hope. She boldly pursued Jesus in order to be made well and whole, and obtained it.

John 5:1-17 tells the story of a man who was an invalid for 38 years. After all that time, he had likely lost hope and more or less settled into the fact that this was how his life would always be. Jesus walked up to him and asked, "Do you want to get well?" The man answers with the reason he's still there, and Jesus brushes that aside and tells him, "Get up! Pick up your mat and walk" (NIV). The man was instantly healed. Jesus saw him among all the others gathered around the pool and healed him. That man may have come to grips with the reality of his situation, but he hadn't lost hope of being made whole.

Mark 5:1-20 tells the story of a demon possessed man that lived in tombs and would run around screaming and cutting himself. Though he had often been chained, he tore the chains apart, and no one could subdue him. No doubt people avoided that place because of him. Jesus cast the demons out, and when everyone showed up, they saw the man "sitting there, dressed and in his right mind" (NIV). The change in that man's life was so dramatic and so powerful that it completely freaked the people out, and they asked Jesus to leave because they were afraid.

Jesus' ministry was, and is, one of hope, healing, and restoration. He sees you. He knows what you need and understands how to bring you closer to Himself. It always amazes me that God knows me best and loves me most. He sees us for who we are right now, but He also knows why we're here. We have a purpose in His kingdom that we are uniquely designed, created, and purposed to fulfill. Jesus is the "how" to being restored and renewed.

In Acts 2 we're told the story of the day of Pentecost. We have to remember that this happened less than two months after Jesus' crucifixion. The people in Jerusalem still remembered the miracles Jesus performed, the fierceness He displayed in the temple, how it felt when He taught in the synagogues, and the brutality of His death. But on this day, the Holy Spirit was given to the believers, and Peter ended up addressing the crowds as they stared and wondered what was going on.

Peter told them that the Messiah had come, and His name was Jesus. He was put to death, but God raised Him back to life and He was now seated on the throne of highest honor at God's right hand. The people were deeply convicted and verse 41 tells us that, "Those who accepted his message were baptized, and about three thousand were added to their number that day." Three thousand people were added to the church in one day! Why? It was the simple message that death had been defeated and Jesus is Lord of all. Jesus was dead, but now He's alive. He offers us that same opportunity.

You were dead because of your sins and because your sinful nature was not yet cut away. Then God made you alive with Christ, for he forgave all our sins. He canceled the record of the charges against us and took it away by nailing it to the cross (Colossians 2:13-14, NLT).

We have to look past who we were and, to a certain degree, the person we are now. We have to keep our eyes fixed on where we're going and on who is guiding us there. I met a guy in a professional development course and, as these things go, we had to introduce ourselves, talk about where we came from, hobbies, etc. This guy refused to speak about where he came from or anything he'd done before. He said, "Where I've been and what I've done have zero bearing on where I'm going." He then proceeded to lay out his career goals and ambitions. It was bold. It was arrogant. It was naïve.

Still, I had to admire the clarity of his vision for where he wanted to go and how he planned to get there.

We've been forgiven and set free from whatever had us bound. Yes, there are many things we need to unlearn. That process colors our spiritual journey and defines some of our struggles, but it has nothing to do with where we're going. Like the old hymn says, "The cross before me, the world behind me..." As long as we're focused on Jesus Christ and listening to the leading of the Holy Spirit, we will be moving forward. Our job is to be willing and obedient in the process.

Discussion Questions

1. What do you love about God? Why?

2. In what area of your life are you asking God for healing, restoration, or freedom?

3. Are you being obedient in the process as Jesus leads you forward?

✦29✦

Men of Action

We make decisions all day long and don't even realize that we're doing it. Let's look at our work day, for example. In order to be at work, you decided at some point that you were actually going to go. You decided to get out of bed and to get dressed. You grabbed your wallet and keys, got into your vehicle, started it, and so on. Tons of little decisions were made, and they all added up to you being at work. It's really not that different when it comes to being a disciple of Jesus Christ. We decide that we're going to follow Him, and then we move forward with purpose.

What good is it, dear brothers and sisters, if you say you have faith but don't show it by your actions? Can that kind of faith save anyone? (James 2:14, NLT)

We are not what we do. What we do is a manifestation of who we are. As we spend time reading the Bible, praying, worshipping, and so on, who we are should be changing to be more reflective of Jesus Christ. I recently saw a bumper sticker that read, "Be the moon, reflect the SON." That's clever, and as I thought about it, I realized that there is some truth being expressed. The moon is positioned so that it reflects the sun, providing us light during the hours of darkness. What I didn't realize is that it not only rotates around the earth once a day, it also makes a full rotation on its axis every day. So, it's not only positioned to reflect the sun, it also moves so that all of it is exposed to the light.

We need to work and position ourselves so that our entire life reflects Christ. We cannot be content with mostly, or even sort of, reflecting Him. We should be putting the effort and energy into exposing more of who we are to Him so every area of our life is seen in His light. Yes, we have decided to follow Jesus, but decision without action is wasted time and energy. We have to be deliberate. We have to be men of action.

Change and education are a given part of our professional life. The more years we have in, the more we're expected to know and the more invested in the organization we should be. We continuously educate ourselves in order to keep up with safety regulations, industry standards, new technology, etc., and we do this as a matter of course. If we don't keep up with the things that matter, then it won't be long until we're replaced by someone who does. Retired US Army General Shinseki once said, "If you dislike change, you're going to dislike irrelevance even more."

In our spiritual life, we can't be content with our current level of understanding and depth of relationship with Jesus. We have to allow Him greater access to all of who we are. Others should be seeing a change in us brought about by God. This is a natural part of being in relationship with Him and should be evident in our life. We have our devotional time, listen to Christian music, go to church, attend small groups, etc., and these are all great things, but are we applying any of it?

One of my nephews went through the rigors of obtaining his private pilot's license. His path wasn't easy as the instructor was hard on him through the different exams and training requirements. For his final solo flight, a camera was placed in the cockpit to record the event, and later he shared the video with family. The entire time he was flying, my nephew narrated what he was doing, how fast he was going, the direction he was headed, and what his next step was going to be. It wasn't just for documentation purposes; it helped remind himself of what he knew and what was important. That young man was focused on completing what he'd worked so hard for and made sure to apply everything he'd read and been taught in order to obtain it.

I'm reminded of Psalm 86:11 and I love how it reads in the

New Living Translation,

> *Teach me your ways, O Lord, that I may live according to your truth! Grant me purity of heart, so that I may honor you.*

The last part of 2 Thessalonians 1:11 says,

> *God will make you worthy of the life to which he called you. And...by His power, will fulfill all your good intentions and faithful deeds* (The Book).

The most powerful example of a Christ-follower is one that's real, honest, true to His nature, and consistently lived. We can never forget that our lives are a reflection of who He is. We have to align our heart's desires with His so that our motivations and intentions for doing things are pleasing to Him. We have to live this out at home, on the job, and at the grocery store because wherever we are, He's there with us. That's right—He's with us everywhere we go, and He knows everything we do. We need to maintain our focus on what's truly important and move forward with purpose.

Discussion Questions

1. Is our spiritual life one of discipleship, or is it just religion?

2. Is our relationship with God part of who we are (brown hair, brown eyes, a disciple of Jesus Christ)?

3. What decisions do you need to make in order to allow Christ to have more of your heart?

❖30❖

Legacy

In Numbers 13, the spies Moses sent out into the Promised Land returned and provided proof of the abundance of crops and gave a report of what they saw to Moses and the people of Israel. The men reported that there were giants in the Promised Land and said that "We seemed like grasshoppers in our own eyes, and we looked the same to them" (Numbers 13:33, NIV).

How we see ourselves matters. The Israelites of that generation couldn't seem to grasp their freedom. If you read Numbers 14, you'll see that the Israelites have a complete breakdown with regards to trusting God. They complained and said things like, "We wish we had died in Egypt" and "Why is the Lord taking us to this country only to have us die in battle? Let us get out of here and return to Egypt!"

The people even wanted to kill Joshua and Caleb because they had nothing but good things to say about the land and were encouraging the people to trust, and not rebel against, God. It's surprising how quickly they discarded everything that God had done for them and how they longed for the familiarity of slavery instead of fighting to attain what God had freed them for.

After this rebellion, God sentenced them to wander in the desert for 40 more years. At the end of that time, the Israelites were again ready to cross into the Promised Land. This time, they're told, "Purify yourselves, for tomorrow the Lord will do great wonders among you" (Joshua 3:5, NLT). When they come to the Jordan River, we're told that,

It was harvest season, and the Jordan was overflowing its banks. But as soon as the feet of the priests who were carrying

the Ark touched the water at the river's edge, the water began piling up at a town upstream… the water below that point flowed on to the Dead Sea until the riverbed was dry (Joshua 3:15-16, The Book).

So the priests were carrying the Ark of the Covenant, and they had to step into the river and start walking across it, even though it was at flood stage. As soon as they moved forward in obedience, the New Living Translation says that the water "began backing up a great distance away." The Israelites didn't know that though. They continued to walk into the river. The farther they walked, the lower and slower the water became, and they stopped once they reached the middle of the river. The priests stood there with the Ark of the Covenant, the symbol of God's presence, while all the people passed by on dry ground.

Are you seeing this?! *As soon as* the Israelites moved forward in faith, in obedience, God stopped the water from flowing. The Israelites had to keep moving forward in faith even though they didn't yet see the physical manifestation of what God had done. It soon became apparent, but God took it a step further. He positioned those who were carrying His presence *in the middle* of the river as a symbol that everyone can safely pass because *He* is right there.

We are pressed on every side by troubles, but we are not crushed. We are perplexed, but not driven to despair. We are hunted down but never abandoned by God. We get knocked down, but we are not destroyed. … For our present troubles are small and won't last very long. Yet they produce for us a glory that vastly outweighs them and will last forever! So we don't look at the troubles we can see now; rather, we fix our gaze on things that cannot be seen. For the things we see now will soon be gone, but the things we cannot see will last forever (2 Corinthians 4:8-9, 17-18, NLT).

Moving forward in faith, even though it looked impossible, enabled the nation of Israel to finally walk into all that God had promised them. We too must continue to press forward even when it seems too risky or too hard, and we're not yet seeing God do anything. The only way to achieve all that He has for us is to keep our head, eyes, and heart focused on Him and *move forward*.

Jesus tells us, "Anyone who puts a hand to the plow and then looks back is not fit for the Kingdom of God" (Luke 9:62, NLT).

Now all glory to God, who is able, through his mighty power at work within us, to accomplish infinitely more than we might ask or think (Ephesians 3:20, NLT).

We are so much more than we realize because of Jesus Christ. How we see ourselves matters. Do we still see ourselves as being in bondage to sin, struggling to get past whatever is holding us back, or do we see ourselves as free, empowered, and protected by the Creator? Christine Caine once said, "So often, we settle for an existence instead of an abundant life, and because of that we are missing out on the adventure God has called us to live! Until we take a leap of faith, we will always wonder, 'What if?'"

When I hear the phrase, "a leap of faith," I tend to think that it applies to other people. I think I'm more of a "shuffle forward in faith" kinda guy. The truth is that my wife and I have made some pretty major decisions in life based on God's leading. We didn't have a clear and precise word from Him for any of it. What we had was a sense in our spirit of what we should or shouldn't do. The direction we were to go in was always confirmed within each other, so we had unity and peace moving forward. Even though things didn't always make sense at the moment, it ultimately became clear that God was protecting and guiding us.

Every decision is a step forward. Each step is movement in a direction. We have to make sure that the direction we're heading in leads us towards what God has for us. We must dare to see ourselves as He does, without the chains that hold us down. The path we travel becomes our story of redemption and sanctification, our legacy. Rest assured, we're going to leave a legacy, and we're building it even now. What will it be?

My sister recently sent me some pictures of my folks at church. My dad was full on worshipping with his hands raised, and the caption read, "Dad doing what he loves best." The picture of my mom was of her embracing another woman while praying over her. I know what being able to do that means to her. When I look back at who they were when I was small and compare it to who they are now, I definitely see the impact of God in their life. Who they are cannot be separated from their faith. I know they've spent their lives pursuing their relationship with God and now, being a husband and father myself, I better understand some of the sacrifices they made.

That's the legacy they're leaving me. What kind of legacy am I leaving for my kids? Is it one of pride and anger, or is it one of faith and obedience? Some of the most important words we'll ever hear are the ones we say to ourselves about ourselves. Jesus Christ will fight *harder* for your heart than anyone else ever will. He will call out parts of your heart that you didn't even know were there.

Jesus came to earth, went through all that He did, and died to save us on purpose. That's not something He would have undertaken if we didn't have immense value or a significant purpose. How we see ourselves matters. We need to listen to His leading and move forward into whatever He's telling us to do, having full confidence that He is with us every step of the way.

Discussion Questions

1   Do you see yourself as small and limited or set free and commissioned by God?

2   God is telling each of us to move forward in faith. What area is that for you and how are you moving forward in it?

3. What kind of legacy are you creating?

→31←

Daring Faith

*Jesus said, "I assure you, even if you had faith as small as a mustard seed you could say to this mountain, 'Move from here to there' and it would move. **Nothing** would be impossible"* (Matthew 17:20, The Book, emphasis mine).

Jesus told His disciples,

Have faith in God. I tell you the truth, you can say to this mountain, "May you be lifted up and thrown into the sea," and it will happen. But you must really believe it will happen and have no doubt in your heart (Mark 11:22-23, NLT).

Those two scriptures really set the bar high. Do you truly believe that you can command a mountain to move? You can't use the "Well, if God told me to say it…" line. You either flat believe it, or you don't. Personally, I don't believe I could. Why? Well, I don't have a reason to tell a mountain to move, but more importantly, I don't think I have the power to do it.

Jesus tells us that whatever we bind on earth is bound in heaven. So, right there I've limited myself. But it has to be possible, or else Jesus wouldn't have told us that we can. He's not prone to exaggeration or anything; He just says what is true. So, why don't we believe that we can do it? Because we don't have faith. If we don't believe we can accomplish something that Jesus plainly told us we could, how can we have bold, courageous, audacious, fearless, walk-on-water faith? I think it starts with one word, "Expect."

When someone asks for our advice, we expect that they'll listen to what we have to say. When we tell our kids to do something, we expect them to do it. We may be wise enough to know

111

that they'll whine a little about it first, but the expectation is that what we've said needs done will be accomplished. When we receive information from our trusted mechanic, we expect that they've correctly diagnosed the problem we identified. When we're given direction at work, it's expected that we'll do whatever it is that we were assigned to do. We recognize our authority and roles in those situations, but do we always recognize the authority we have through Jesus?

A Roman centurion came to Jesus, asking for his servant to be healed. Jesus says that he'll come and will heal the boy. The centurion stops him and says,

> *It isn't necessary for you to come. If you will only stand here and say, "Be healed," my servant will get well! I know, because I am under the authority of my superior officers and I have authority over my soldiers, and I say to one, "Go," and he goes, and to another, "Come," and he comes, and to my slave boy, "Do this or that," and he does it. And I know you have authority to tell his sickness to go—and it will go!* (Matthew 8:5-13, TLB)

In Matthew 28:18, Jesus tells us that He's been given all power and authority in heaven and on earth. He also said that if we ask anything in His name, it would be done. So, what's my hang-up with telling a mountain to get up and move? Jesus told us we can do it, so what's the problem?

I get focused on the physicality of it all—it's a mountain. These geological formations are created by shifting tectonic plates, which means that they're actually part of the earth's surface, not like a rock or a scoop of sand at the beach. They are permanently connected, massive sections of the earth's mantle. If you think six yards of dirt is heavy, think about the weight of the nearly 5.5 miles of rock that make up Mt. Everest. The real issue is that I'm looking at what I see, and it doesn't seem possible. I'm limiting my abilities in the spiritual realm based solely on what I see in the physical.

"I am the Lord," he says, "and there is no other. I publicly pro-claim bold promises. I do not whisper obscurities in some dark corner so on one can understand what I mean. And I did not tell the people of Israel to ask me for something I did not plan to give. I, the Lord, speak only what is true and right" (Isaiah 45:18-19, The Book).

With God, it's not a matter of "expect"; it's a guarantee. He wouldn't tell us we could do something if it weren't true. If He says we can move mountains, then they're there, waiting for us to move them. Each of us has been given authority through Jesus' name. We need to recognize this! That authority comes with strings attached, though. We have to be aligned with His will and His plan when we exercise it.

One of the jobs I once had was the deputy for facilities related functions in a large, technology-based building. When my boss was out, it was my job to keep things running smoothly. One time, he was gone for a couple weeks, and a guy approached me with a proposal that would've changed several things. He spelled it all out, and what he wanted to do made a lot of sense to me. But I knew that my boss would not approve of the changes, so I vetoed it. The guy became really frustrated with me and said, "Why won't you do this? I know you get it!" My response was, "It's not my show. I'm just minding the store for the boss, and we both know he wouldn't approve this."

It's the same way in our relationship with Jesus! We are to take on His vision and execute His plan. I don't know what's best for me, but I know He does. I know that He set me on the path of righteousness and will keep me securely there. I need to do things His way. It's just that simple.

If you want to know what God wants you to do, ask him, for he is always ready to give a bountiful supply of wisdom to all who ask him (James 1:5, TLB).

We need to ask God what we should do, where we should go, and even what we should pray for.

When you ask him, be sure that you really expect him to answer, for a doubtful mind is as unsettled as a wave of the sea that is driven and tossed by the wind. People like that should not expect to receive anything from the Lord. They can't make up their minds. They waver back and forth in everything they do (James 1:6-8, The Book).

We have to *expect* that He'll answer us. When He does, we need to accept what God has told us and act on it.

If we're aligned with His heart, then we'll ask for, say, and do, the right things in the right way—the way that pleases His heart. If we're doing His will, we'll properly exercise the authority He's bestowed upon us. We cannot be timid in accomplishing whatever He's given us to do. We must go forward with all the boldness and courage that come from carrying out the commands of *the* Creator.

Discussion Questions

1. In what areas of your spiritual life do you feel that you lack authority?

2. With what areas of your life are you not trusting God?

3. Why do you not have trust or faith that He will take care of you in that area?

⤙32⤚

Own It

Our church helped build a school in India and sent over clothes, shoes, and backpacks stuffed with school supplies for the children. In a video made of the event, we could see a little girl that had just put on her new shoes carefully tuck her feet up under her. She had this look on her face that I recognized from my own kids. It was a look that said, "I feel special now." I also felt the excitement and joy of one little boy as he opened up his backpack of school supplies. Later in the service, I saw someone who had been going through hard times for a number of years with their hands raised in worship. It was very evident from the tears coursing down their face and their expression that they were communicating with the Father.

Each of these moments was beautiful in its own way, and I was emotionally impacted by them all. However, the experience I had was secondhand. I was watching someone else's experience and had no ownership of it. It was, after all, their moment.

Joshua led the nation of Israel into the Promised Land, and we're told that

The people had remained true to the Lord throughout Joshua's lifetime, and as long afterward as the old men of his generation were still living—those who had seen the mighty miracles the Lord had done for Israel. But finally all that generation died, and the next generation did not worship Jehovah as their God and did not care about the mighty miracles he had done for Israel. They did many things that the Lord had expressly forbidden, including the worshiping of heathen gods (Judges 2:7,10-11, TLB).

It's amazing to realize that in just *one* generation, the nation of Israel goes from worshipping God and honoring Him completely to being a people that incurred God's anger because of their idol worship. What changed? Why did that happen? Did the parents not pass on the laws God gave them? Did they not teach their children well? I think it's because the kids decided not to enter into their own relationship with God.

I look at my life and see the same thing. I was raised in a Christian home; my folks had a definite relationship with God, and they sought Him out in very real ways. As an adolescent and as a young man, I didn't want that. I wanted to do what I wanted, and I sought those things out. Just like He did for the nation of Israel in the Old Testament, God warned me of His coming judgment. I knew it was coming if I didn't turn around, and it rattled me. I didn't obey and reaped what I had sown.

So, my experience with God is very real, very personal, very deep. There's no way I can pass that experience and closeness forged in battle on to my kids any more than my parents could with me. What can I do? Lead.

If you notice, the Israelites didn't turn away from God until those who had experienced God in the desert and in battle had died. The "old guard" set the tone in word and deed. Words alone ain't gonna get it done. We have to be *doing* it. We can't *make* our kids have a relationship with Jesus. But we can show them what it looks like when they do, and they should be able to see and feel a difference in us because of it.

I loved watching my son play when he was very young. He has a vivid imagination, and he creates his own world. Whatever he was playing with was very real to him at the moment. As I would watch, I could tell by his expressions, words, and actions how intense the experience was for him. It's quite remarkable actually. I've also watched him sit for hours with a box of little Lego pieces and a book that provides step-by-step instructions on how to build something. I've flipped through those books, looked at the steps, and have seen the final product, but I don't have a sense of pride in the building sitting on his nightstand.

Why? I didn't rummage through a box looking for just the right piece to put in the right place at the right time in order to create that building. I didn't experience the frustration of trying to make certain pieces fit together correctly. I didn't feel the panic when a tiny, but crucial, piece was dropped, and it bounced under the couch with the dog in close pursuit. So I don't know the pride and satisfaction he felt when the completed structure was presented with all the flair of a lost Picasso being unveiled for the first time.

"Be ye doers of the word, and not hearers only…" (James 1:22, KJV). The experience is founded in the doing.

Matthew 16:13-21 tells us the story of Jesus asking His disciples about those who followed Him from town to town and who they said He is. Their answers were a mixed bag of Old Testament prophets and even John the Baptist. When Jesus asked the disciples about who He is, Peter declared that He is "the Messiah, the Son of the living God."

I'm sure there were many in the crowds that had been to most of the places Jesus had gone. They had seen many of the same things the disciples did; they likely appreciated the miracles and the strength of Jesus' teaching. But the people in the crowd didn't own the experience in the same way the disciples did. The people wanted to see signs and miracles. They wanted to be entertained. The disciples left their families, their jobs—everything—in order to follow Jesus. They wanted to be with Him, to do life with Him, and to experience *who* He is.

Jesus has asked each of us, "Who am I to you?" but do we ever ask Him, "Who am I in You? Who do You see me to be?" Colossians 3:3 tells us that our true life is "hidden with Christ in God" (NLT).

God will,

Give to each one (who is victorious) a white stone, and on the stone will be engraved a new name that no one understands except the one who receives it (Revelations 2:17, NLT).

That stone has our *God-given* identity engraved on it. He knows the person you're supposed to be. He knows how to take you from where you are to where you should be. We need to seek that level of familiarity in our relationship with Christ so that He will be able to guide us there.

Discussion Questions

1. If asked, who would you say Jesus is to you?

2. How are you owning your walk with Christ?

3. When God gives you insight as to your identity in Him, do you latch onto it as truth?

⇢33⇠

Amos 4:11

I was reading the book of Amos, and in chapter 4 God details for the nation of Israel the things He's done in an effort to show them their need for Him, but sadly they refused to listen. Verse 11 says,

> *"I destroyed some of your cities, as I destroyed Sodom and Gomorrah. Those of you who survived were like charred sticks pulled from a fire. But still you would not return to me,"* says the Lord (NLT).

Most of us have done the campfire thing at least once in our lives so you probably know what a stick looks like when you pull it out after it's been in the fire for a bit. It's blackened, burnt, and really not good for much other than throwing it back in the fire to finish burning. God is comparing what He's done to some people in order to get their attention to that burnt stick! That's powerful imagery!

I once visited a state park that had been completely burned the year prior. The grasses and wildflowers came back with a vengeance and covered the hillsides. Many of the trees were recovering from the wildfire, but some were too badly damaged to do so. Those that survived still bore the scars from being burnt just the year before. Over time, new growth will cover that damaged area, and unless you were aware of what had happened, you'd never know what that tree had been through just by looking at it.

We took our kids to a museum/science center kind of place, and one of the exhibits was a gargantuan section of tree that was several hundred years old. By examining the growth rings, a dendrologist was able to determine the tree's age and, to a certain degree, chronicle its life. Sections in the growth rings were pointed out that corresponded to key points in human history. Other sections showed periods of severe drought, heavy rainfall, and different wildfires that ravaged the forest in which the tree grew. It was extremely interesting to be able to learn so much just by looking at those growth rings. Had we come across that tree in the woods or a field, we would've admired its size and wondered at how old it is. However, until its growth rings are examined, nobody would know what it had been through.

It occurs to me that our lives are very similar. We've all walked through things and have been through the fire in one way or another. We bear the scars of who we were and the person we made ourselves into. If you were to examine any one of our lives like the rings on that tree, you'd see seasons of growth, seasons of famine, and the scars of more extreme times. On top of those scars, you should also see healing, renewal, and growth brought about by the Holy Spirit. If we are truly seeking a deeper relationship with Jesus Christ, then the Holy Spirit will be talking to us about things in our life that don't belong there.

God isn't an accuser who points out something in your life and then laughs at you for it. He puts His finger on an area in order to identify it, then brings healing and restoration. "Who" we are should constantly be re-defined, refined, and purified in such a way that we're different today compared to who we were last week, last month, last year. We *have* to be! Our families are counting on us! It's not about having a powerful testimony or an influential ministry. Second only to our relationship with God, we're supposed to lovingly *serve* our family!

We define what a father is for our kids. I know a guy that loves the Lord and loves to enter into worship. He talks about "practicing the presence of God." I'm not sure what that means exactly, but I do know that this brother definitely feels it. As much as he loves Jesus and seeks His presence, he struggles with the concept of

"God the Father" because his own dad was so abusive.

What kind of example are we setting? It doesn't matter how old your kids are or where they're at in the world, what we're doing *now* matters. They're still watching us. Believe it! Are they seeing a difference in us? Is our parenting pleasing to God? Is the way we love and serve our wives pleasing to God?

Praying over each member of our family has a huge impact on how we interact, relate, and love each person. By bringing them before the throne of God in prayer, we learn what matters to God about each one regardless of what season they're in. Only then will we be better positioned to love them as they need to be loved. The more often I pray over my wife, the more I see her differently, and the deeper my love is for her. The more I pray for the child that's too much like me for my own good, the more patient and understanding I am with them. The more I pray over the child that I don't understand as well, the better I understand them and the more loving I am with them. It is *God* who is changing my heart for my family.

God didn't redeem us, set us free, and set us on the path of righteousness only to leave us there. We're to constantly move forward with Him. He's in charge, and He's leading us where we need to go. All we have to do is stay close so we don't get lost. If you think about it, that totally takes the pressure off of us, doesn't it?

With regards to our family, we don't leave them behind either. We're also supposed to be out in front of our family, leading them, fighting the enemy, and clearing a path for them to follow. Are we doing that? Talk is cheap, and hollow deeds of service are as desirable as a tall glass of warm, chunky, spoiled milk. There's a spirit that accompanies our every word and deed. What "vibe" are we putting off at home? The rubber meets the road at home. Our marital status, how many kids are living at home, or even how old they are doesn't matter. What matters is whether or not we are living to please God in all that we say and do.

Discussion Questions

1. Is the example you're setting pleasing to His heart?

2. As you pursue Christ, how are you caring for your family and loved ones differently?

3. How does praying over your family and loved ones change how you see and treat them?

✣34✣

Joy

Many things in life try to steal our joy—even little things like getting pickles on your burger even though you specifically said, "No pickles, please." There are also assaults on our life that make our world become small and consume us mentally and emotionally. I've been there and struggled with "Why is this happening?" There are times when even simple things seem harder than they should be. Is life just that hard? Is it just our luck that everything seems to be difficult when it should be easy?

It's none of those things. As I see it, trials and hardships come along for two reasons: 1) poor decision making, and 2) they are there to refine and purify us.

Trust in the Lord with all your heart; do not depend on your own understanding. Seek his will in all you do, and he will direct your paths (Proverbs 3:5-6, The Book).

It's easy to trust God with the big decisions and the big problems. Usually, the situation or issue is so deep and complex that we can't sort it out on our own. It only makes sense to seek help when faced with the big stuff. So, we turn to God. But what about the little stuff? Do we still ask for His guidance and listen for His voice in the more mundane things?

One year my family planned to visit relatives during Thanksgiving time. Initially, we were going to drive, but it was an 875 mile, 15-hour jaunt across six states just to get there. We planned to break the drive up over two days so it wasn't too hard on the kids, and even factored in staying at a hotel with an indoor pool so they could get their energy out. The bummer was that amount of driving, roundtrip, was going to cut the time of our visit in half. We'd be spending the same number of days driving as we would visiting. Not ideal.

Now, my wife is a great bargain shopper so she took this on as a personal challenge and jumped on the internet. She was able to secure plane tickets that were slightly more expensive than the cost of our roundtrip drive. No-brainer, right? We bought the tickets and anxiously looked forward to our trip. We later realized that we hadn't prayed about the decision. I failed to heed Proverbs 3:7 which advises, "Don't be impressed with your own wisdom" (The Book). As it turned out, our flights were canceled due to weather conditions, and we ended up driving anyway. Really should've prayed about that.

God tells us, "Look! I am the Eternal, the God of all living things. Is anything too difficult for Me?" (Jeremiah 32:27, Voice)

So, why don't we trust Him with more? That's the topic of many a sermon, but the bottom line is that because we don't, it causes us unnecessary hardships and costs us some of our joy and contentment. Trials and hardships are sometimes consequences of our decisions, but they also come along to refine and purify us.

Prophesying about Jesus, Isaiah says,

He was despised and rejected—a man of sorrows, acquainted with the deepest grief. We turned our backs on him and looked the other way. He was despised, and we did not care. Yet it was our weaknesses he carried; it was our sorrows that weighed him down. And we thought his troubles were a punishment from God, a punishment for his own sins! But he was pierced for our rebellion, crushed for our sins. He was beaten so we could be whole. He was whipped so we could be healed. All of us, like sheep, have strayed away. We have left God's paths to follow our own. Yet the Lord laid on him the sins of us all. He was oppressed and treated harshly, yet he never said a word. He was led like a lamb to the slaughter. And as a sheep is silent before the shearers, he did not open his mouth (Isaiah 53:3-7, NLT).

*And it was right and proper that God, who made everything for his own glory, should allow Jesus to suffer, for in doing this he was bringing vast multitudes of God's people to heaven; for his suffering made Jesus a **perfect** Leader, one fit to bring them into their salvation* (Hebrews 2:10, TLB, emphasis mine).

Everything that Jesus went through reinforced His relationship, faith, trust—His reliance on the Father. There are some things that keep popping up in our lives, and they're no fun at all. We sit and shake our heads and ask, "Why Lord?! Why is this so hard?" What we should be saying is, "Lord, I'd love to move forward; to move off of this spot. Please show me what I need to learn and help me retain the lesson."

In 2 Corinthians 12:7, Paul says that in order to keep him humble he "was given a physical condition which has been a thorn in my flesh, a messenger from Satan to hurt and bother me and prick my pride" (TLB). Paul didn't accept whatever his "thorn" was as part of his character or part of his life. God tells him in verse 9 that, "My grace is sufficient for you, my power is made perfect in weakness." He came to understand that his thorn served a purpose in his life, and he accepted God's use of it. The things that are a constant struggle aren't there to shame us. They're there to drive us to God!

Luke 7:36-50 tells the story of a sinful woman who is broken and repentant at Jesus' feet. It's a beautiful and powerful story and in verse 47 Jesus said, "I tell you, her sins—and they are many—have been forgiven, so she has shown me much love" (NLT).

That woman did not experience a trite "attitude of gratitude." She knew what she had been forgiven of and loved the One who had set her free. She had a deep understanding that what was received is not what was deserved. Jesus was brutalized and killed to pay the penalty for our sins. The fact that we've been set free, all by itself, should bring about such a deep sense of gratitude that we live our lives in such a way that we seek to be worthy of the sacrifice He made. That gratitude should be so profound that it causes a foundational shift in our lives. *Jesus* is the source of our joy.

"The Lord has done great things for us and we are filled with joy" (Psalm 126:3, NIV).

> *I have loved you even as the Father has loved me. Live within my love. When you obey me you are living in my love, just as I obey my Father and live in his love. I have told you this so that you will be filled with my joy. Yes, your cup of joy will overflow!* (John 15:9-11, TLB)

We need to keep our focus on Christ and live within His love. Only then will we know true joy. *He* is the source of life. *He* is the one who rescued us. *He* knows us better and loves us more than anyone ever will.

Discussion Questions

1. What decisions do you make (or keep making) that cost you joy and contentment?

2. How can we let go of things that we've long held on to and increase our reliance on God?

3. What does it mean to you to "live within" Jesus' love?

⇥35↤

Change

God has been impressing upon me that I need to take better care of myself. I haven't been eating right or exercising enough, and as a result, I started gaining weight. I've made a few changes and have lost a couple of pounds. I can't say that I'm proud of that or that I've accomplished anything because really and truly—I haven't. Changing a couple habits and dropping a couple pounds isn't "nothing," but compared to what I felt God was telling me to do, it definitely falls short.

So why haven't I been obedient? The honest answer is that in order to make real and significant changes, I will have to be uncomfortable. I will have to change my routines and do things differently. I will have to do things that shine a light on my weaknesses; might hurt a little but will ultimately cause me to be stronger. I know the changes God wants me to make are needed; they are for my good and will enable me to accomplish things He has for me to do. So why am I not doing them?

I was talking with someone recently and was calling out the promise on their life. They looked at me incredulously, and I answered their unasked question by saying, "You're wondering how I know these things. It's because I see you differently than you see yourself."

I remember becoming aware of how I defined myself. I was sharing a story of something that had happened, and as the conversation went on, I heard how I was describing myself to others. My words didn't feel right even as I spoke them. I was defining myself in a way that was not who I am; it was the person I used to be. Is our picture of ourselves accurate? Is that who God says we are? The truth is, unless our self-definition begins with "I am a child of God," then we've got it wrong.

Temptation comes from the lure of our own evil desires. These evil desires lead to evil actions, and evil actions lead to death (James 1:14-15, The Book).

In that passage, there is an implicit agreement that we make with the temptation or sin that's trying to gain a foothold. Sin first requires us to agree that it's a good idea. Whether it's milliseconds or days, some degree of planning goes into executing that idea, and then there's deliberate action in making it happen.

In his book *Truly Free*, Pastor Robert Morris says,

The good news is that regardless of what difficulty you're struggling with today, there is always hope. Sure, the temptation never quite goes away in this life. There is always a pull towards thoughts and actions that could cause us to become burdened again by a yoke of slavery. But you need to know—and live out fully—that you never need to return to (slavery).

We don't *have* to obey the call of our sinful desires! We've been released from those bonds and are free to choose differently, to choose Christ! We can also choose to go back into bondage to our anger, to porn, to overeating, to substance abuse, or whatever it may be, but we don't *have* to.

I remember not knowing how to think differently. The only action, reaction, or response I knew in many situations was one tied to anger. One day I was in the middle of something and was about to step foot on that well-traveled path when God showed me that I didn't *have* to get angry at that moment. I was about to pick it, but I didn't have to. That was huge for me!

We have to be willing to be uncomfortable. We need to understand that some things we've said and done for a long time are no longer acceptable. We may understand what needs to be done, and we may understand the steps involved, but if we're not willing to actually change and grow, then all of that understanding means nothing. Sure, we want to be different, but we have to do what's necessary to actually make the changes.

Jesus said to all of his followers, "If you truly desire to be my disciple, you must disown your life completely, embrace my 'cross' as your own, and surrender to my ways" (Luke 9:23, TPT).

We have to stop agreeing with the temptations and wrong desires in our lives. We have to ignore their cries to be fed and choke them out. We have to see ourselves as capable of being different and make the choices that take us in that direction. We have to see ourselves as free from whatever held us in bondage and take deliberate steps to stay away from those things. We have to know that Jesus set us free from all of that and know that we *never* have to go back to it.

This is not a "self-help" kind of message. This is not some New Age doctrine of "the good within" or some other bit of utter nonsense. The truth is that if I had some greater good within, then I would not have said and done the things I did. If I could've fixed myself, I would've. But I couldn't. I needed Jesus to come in and rescue me from who and where I was. The truth of the matter is that I *still* don't know what's best for me. I'm so thankful that Jesus Christ does.

Jesus said, "Just as Moses lifted up the snake in the wilderness, so the Son of Man must be lifted up, that everyone who believes may have eternal life in him" (John 3:14, NIV).

Jesus was referring to when the Israelites began grumbling and complaining against God and His provision in their lives, so He sent poisonous snakes among them as a form of punishment. After the people repented, God told Moses to, "Make a replica of a poisonous snake and attach it to the top of a pole. Those who are bitten will live if they simply look at it!" (Numbers 21:8, The Book)

When I read that, so many things come together at once—the serpent lying to Eve in the Garden of Eden and bringing spiritual death to mankind; serpents bringing physical death to the Israelites; having to look up at the cause of their suffering nailed to a pole and being restored; Jesus being nailed to the cross, taking on the sins of the world, crushing sin, and death forever, and setting us free.

We will live, we will have life, and we will accomplish *all* that He has for us if we keep our eyes focused on the cross and accept all of what Christ did for us there.

You are slaves of sin, every one of you. And slaves don't have rights, but the Son has every right there is! So, if the Son sets you free, you will indeed be free (John 8:34-36, TLB).

True heart change is brought about by God, but we have to willingly cooperate in that change. We usually see ourselves as being less than the person He sees us to be. Jesus did not leave heaven, come to earth as a baby, endure all the suffering He did, and die a horrible death just so we could continue to struggle with anger, lust, selfishness, pride, unforgiveness, and so on. Each one of us is better acquainted with our struggles and failures than we'd like to be. We need to accept the fact that we don't *have* to be that person in any way, ever again. We can choose to do so, but we don't have to. We need to define ourselves as sons of the Living God and walk in all that means.

Discussion Questions

1. What area of your life are you still being disobedient in?
2. What do you need to do in order to move forward with what God is asking of you?
3. Do you see yourself as having been truly set free?

⇥36⇤

Zechariah 7

On December 7 of the fourth year of King Darius's reign, another message came to Zechariah from the Lord. The people of Bethel had sent Sharezer and Regemmelech, along with their attendants, to seek the Lord's favor. They were to ask this question of the prophets and the priests at the Temple of the Lord of Heaven's Armies: "Should we continue to mourn and fast each summer on the anniversary of the Temple's destruction, as we have done for so many years?" (Zechariah 7:1-3, NLT).

I read that and I immediately wondered, "Who told them to fast in the first place? What was the purpose of the fast? If this fast was commanded by God, wouldn't He cancel it when it was time? Why were they asking if they still had to do it?" So, I did a bit of research and discovered that this period of mourning and fasting had become a tradition to mark the destruction of the Temple. In fact, it is still observed in the Jewish culture today as *Tisha B'Av* (literally translates to the "9th of Av."). This observance now incorporates many other tragedies that occurred, but it was primarily meant to commemorate the destruction of the temple by Nebuchadnezzar.

The Israelites in exile practiced this period of mourning, fasting, and abstinence for 70 years. The thing that strikes me is that they weren't mourning their sins, their idolatry, or their stubborn refusal to repent and turn to God. They weren't sorry that their rebelliousness caused God to turn them over to their enemies and that they suffered mightily because of it. Ezekiel 10 even describes the glory of God leaving the temple, leaving Jerusalem. Yet even this abandonment wasn't the cause of their mourning. After having suffered starvation and disease during the siege of Jerusalem, the brutal killing of many people, the cruel treatment and forced removal from the Promised Land, they *still* didn't acknowledge what they had done nor did they repent for their sins. Instead, they mourned the destruction of a building.

> *God then tells them, "Tell all the people of the land and the priests, 'When you fasted and mourned in the fifth and seventh months these past 70 years, did you really do it for me? When you ate and drank, didn't you do it to benefit yourselves? Aren't these the same words that the Lord announced through the earlier prophets when Jerusalem and its surrounding cities were inhabited and undisturbed and the Negev and the foothills were still inhabited?'"* (Zechariah 7:5-7, GW)

For 70 years, they got it wrong. It wasn't about God; it was about them. I can see how it started out with good intentions, but at the end of the day, their heart wasn't right in doing it. Each one of us goes about life doing things we understand we should do. We also do things we should without understanding why. I have to ask, are we doing what we're doing for the right reasons?

We used to go to a large church, and I was on one of the teams there. As a founding member of that team, I helped develop our procedures and had a fair amount of responsibility. It would be an understatement to say that I was invested. As a team, we were there quite a bit, maybe too much in retrospect. Overall, I had a firm understanding of our true purpose and enjoyed what I was doing on a lot of levels.

Then one day when I was serving, I noticed that my heart wasn't right. I hadn't done anything wrong, but my heart was no longer positioned properly. I had gotten caught up in the functional aspects of serving and allowed the real reason we were there to slip away. At that moment, I knew I had to step down. I did not want to be doing the right thing for the wrong reasons. The further

I go in my walk with Christ, the more I realize what a big deal my heart's position is.

In the military, there's a phrase that's used in marching or standing in a formation—"cover and align." In this context, to "cover" means to be directly behind the person in front of you. To "align" means that one should be positioned on the same lateral plane as the person to your left and right. The intent is that individuals aren't seen, but rather it's the group that is seen as it moves in unison of purpose and direction. I want to be covered and aligned with God. I don't want to be seen. Ever. I want my desires, efforts, and accomplishments to be completely in sync with His intent.

Each one of us has things God has put on our hearts to do. We need to listen to His voice and follow His leading as we work to move forward in the direction He's given us. We may not understand the "why" behind what we're asked to do, but are we being obedient? Are we working to position ourselves for what's next? Are we testing what's being said to us and spoken over us by others to see if they line up with what we know He's already placed in our heart? Do all of these things align with His Word?

We must be careful that we're accomplishing His will and plan for our lives and not someone else's. We need to examine ourselves to be sure that all we say and do, as well as the "why" behind it, are a direct reflection of who God is.

Discussion Questions

1. Examine yourself. What is your true heart attitude behind the things that you do and in the way that you do them?

2. Are the things you're doing (serving your family, serving others, etc.) being done in a way that pleases His heart?

3. How will you submit those things to God and align yourself with His will?

✦37✦

Holy

So think clearly and exercise self-control. Look forward to the special blessings that will come to you at the return of Jesus Christ. Obey God because you are his children. Don't slip back into your old ways of doing evil: you didn't know any better then. But now you must be holy in everything you do, just as God—who chose you to be his children—is holy. For he himself has said, "You must be holy because I am holy" (1 Peter 1:13-16, The Book).

Numbers 18:1-5 tells us that the Levites were selected by God to assist the priests in serving at the tabernacle, and they were to perform all the duties related to the physical structure of the tabernacle. So, Leviticus was written to provide instructions to the nation of Israel, but more specifically, it was a type of handbook for the Levites. God made that decree about His people being holy because He is holy five times in the book of Leviticus.

I am the Lord your God; consecrate yourselves and be holy, because I am holy. ...I am the Lord, who brought you up out of Egypt to be your God; therefore be holy, because I am holy (Leviticus 11:44-45, NIV).

Speak to the entire assembly of Israel and say to them: "Be holy because I, the Lord your God, am holy" (Leviticus 19:2, NIV).

Consecrate yourselves and be holy, because I am the Lord your God. You are to be holy to me because I, the Lord, am holy, and I have set you apart from the nations to be my own (Leviticus 20:7,26 NIV).

Keep my commands and follow them. I am the Lord. Do not profane my holy name, for I must be acknowledged as holy by the Israelites. I am the Lord, who made you holy and who brought you out of Egypt to be your God. I am the Lord (Leviticus 22:31-33, NIV).

I grabbed our *Webster's New International Dictionary* to look up "holy" and it is defined as, "set apart to the service or worship of a deity; hallowed; sacred." Now, that particular edition was published in 1934; it weighs around 15 lbs and is 6-7" thick. Out of curiosity, I did an internet search for "holy," and Merriam-Webster.com currently defines it as, "exalted or worthy of complete devotion as one perfect in goodness and righteousness; divine." Not quite the same, is it? Things come and go in our society. Our priorities change, we change what is acceptable, and we even change the meaning of words to reinforce society's new views and values. But the Bible is full of passages declaring that God never changes and neither do His words.

What does this mean for you and me? First Peter 2:9, Revelations 1:6, and 5:10 all tell us that *we* are God's Kingdom; *we* are His priests! So, His instructions to the Levites apply to us today. *You* are a priest in your home. *You* represent the Lord *your* God when you're at work or at the store. Are we doing it well? Are we doing it accurately? God's laws were never intended to be a burden or something rigidly adhered to. They are there to point us to life. That life is Jesus Christ.

Jesus told His disciples, "If you love me, obey my command-ments. Those who obey my commandments are the ones who love me. All those who love me will do what I say" (John 14:15,21, 23, The Book).

As we're raising our kids, we teach them basic rules when they're little, and we expand the scope of those rules as they grow and mature. Our goal is that they become a person of godly character. We want them to grow in understanding, intuitively know right from wrong, and make choices that are in agreement with the Holy Spirit.

When they're old enough to know better, and they deliberately break the rules, we may get angry, but what we're really feeling is a sense of hurt and betrayal because our child chose to defy us. In some instances, it just feels personal and we think, *Wow, I thought you loved me more than to talk to me like that* or *I thought you loved me more than to act like that when you're not in my presence.* Jesus is saying the same thing to us, "If you love me, keep my commands."

King David understood what God wanted and he wrote,

You would not be pleased with sacrifices, or I would bring them. If I brought you a burnt offering, you would not accept it. The sacrifice you want is a broken spirit. A broken and repentant heart, O God, you will not despise (Psalm 51:16-17, The Book).

God said,

If my people, who are called by my name, will humble themselves and pray and seek my face and turn from their wicked ways, then will I hear from heaven and will forgive their sin and heal their land (2 Chronicles 7:14, NIV).

Our call to holiness is extended by Jesus Christ Himself. The good news is that we don't have to worry about becoming holy or even being holy. Why? Because we attain holiness, not by adhering to a complex set of rules, but by accepting Jesus as our Lord and by having a relationship with our loving God. As we pursue a deeper relationship with Him, He will guide and direct our paths and keep us steady through life's storms. He will accomplish the refining work of making us holy. Our job is simply to be willing and obedient.

Discussion Questions

1. How does your interpretation of "holy" line up with God's?

2. How do we go about becoming more holy?

3. How is God's holiness being made manifest in your life on a day-to-day basis.

→38←

1 Peter 5:8

I was watching a nature show the other day, and the program was about how lions hunt and survive in Africa. It so happened that a herd of Cape buffalo were near a lion pride, and the lead female lion was watching them, looking for which buffalo she could attack and kill. A young calf began wandering away from its mother and the herd, and the lion immediately noticed it. The lion briefly watched and then began stalking the calf, creeping forward until she was within striking distance.

Suddenly, she sprinted out of the grass and swatted the calf with a swing powerful enough to potentially break its back. The lioness sank her one inch long claws into the calf's flesh then grabbed it by the neck with her two-and-a-half inch long teeth, pinning it to the ground. The calf was wild-eyed and bleating pitifully from fear and pain. The lion was merciless, pausing only to adjust its bite deeper into the calf's neck. The scene was either horrifying or beautiful depending on your viewpoint and sensitivities, but it was brutally straightforward regardless of which way you look at it.

Be alert and of sober mind. Your enemy the devil prowls around like a roaring lion looking for someone to devour (1 Peter 5:8, NIV).

Gentlemen, *we* are Satan's prey. He watches us, looking for someone weak of heart, someone taking a nap spiritually, someone not where they should be, and he attacks. He may stalk you a bit, baiting you with "lesser" sins, but make no mistake—the goal is always to knock you down, bite you in the neck, and consume you while you're still crying out in fear and pain. As guys, we may look at that and say, "You want a piece of me? Fine. Bring it!" The thing is, he's not just after us. He's after your wife. He's after your kids.

We have to realize that we are engaged in a 24/7 battle. If you think I'm exaggerating, look around. As an example, on my way to church I pass billboards where pictures of juicy burgers, crispy fries, and a cold soda call out to me. There's one that provides an update of the current lottery jackpots, and there was another with the image of a young lady dressed in such a way that I'm really not sure what product was being advertised. So, over the course of a ten-minute drive to church, there's a battle being waged for my attention and affection in the areas of health, finance, and purity. We won't even get into the commercials on TV or what's being shown as "family" programming these days. We can't live under a rock, and we can't become separatists living on a compound somewhere. So, what can we do? We dig in and we fight.

We have to recognize that the spiritual world is *more* real than the physical world we live in. The spiritual world can impact and affect the physical world, but the only way to impact the spiritual world is through prayer. It's not enough to have a belief in God, go to church, and listen to a Christian radio station sometimes.

Do you still think it's enough just to believe that there is one God? Well, even the demons believe this, and they tremble in terror! (James 2:19, The Book).

The truth is that we *are* at war. Every decision you and I make determines whether ground is gained or lost. Again, there's no exaggeration here.

Temptation comes from the lure of our own evil desires. These evil desires lead to evil actions, and evil actions lead to death (James 1:14-15, The Book).

Every desire, *every* thought, and *every* action are connected. They are all steps in a given direction. Where are those desires, thoughts, and actions leading us? What are we focusing on? *Who* are we listening to and whom are we following?

Earlier I said that we need to fight, and we do. The question is how? We can flail about in any given direction, but we need to focus our energy and attack in a dedicated manner. It starts with the simple understanding of what Christ did on the cross. He set us free—simply because He loves us. If we don't understand the magnitude of that, then we're missing the entire point.

We're no longer condemned to be the person Satan wants us to be. We don't *have* to participate in our own destruction. We don't have to make those same choices. Like a locust that molts and sheds its skin, we've been released from the confines of that old life. Like a butterfly, we're changed, transformed, and are able to do the things that we were truly designed, created, and purposed for.

I am the Lord... and there is no other. I publicly proclaim bold promises. I do not whisper obscurities in some dark corner so no one can understand what I mean. And I did not tell the people of Israel to ask me for something I did not intend to give. I, the Lord, speak only what is true and right (Isaiah 45: 18-19, The Book).

Jesus said, "You can ask for anything in my name, and I will do it, so that the Son can bring glory to the Father. Yes, ask me for anything in my name, and I will do it!" (John 14:13-14, NLT)

When I take a shower, I have to turn the water on for a little bit so the cold water runs out, and the hot water comes in. But, it's not that way with God. We have the full power, strength, might, mercy, and love—all of who God is—available to us 100% of the time. Do we take advantage of what He is offering us? Anything and everything else is false. It's fake. It will lure us away from where we should be—away from God—and we'll be attacked. We don't ever really get a day off. We *are* being stalked.

The calf I mentioned at the opening did not die. It was saved by its mother. The Cape buffalo is fierce, aggressive, and has no love for the lion. Like, none. The calf's wounds will heal, but it will forever bear the marks of that attack. The calf will never forget what it felt like to be vulnerable and in the clutches of the lion. It will never forget what the lion smelled like, and when it catches so much as a whiff of lion breath in the air, that calf will react and alert the rest of the herd.

That attack may not have killed the calf, but its awareness and reactions were forever altered. What was meant for harm will now help protect the herd. In the same way, we must turn to Jesus so what was meant to harm and destroy us will be used to protect our families and each other.

Discussion Questions

1. Do you live like Satan is watching you, looking for an opportunity to tempt you and bring you down?

2. Do you cover your family in prayer and protect them spiritually in a meaningful way?

3. Do you believe that your prayers are effective? If not, why?

✦39✦

The Leper

In Luke 6:27-34, Jesus tells us to love our enemies. He tells us that we should pray for those who hate us, treat us poorly, abuse us, persecute us, and take things from us. To be honest, I never liked this particular teaching. To me, Jesus was saying, "Be a doormat. Shut up and take it. Whatever it is, just shut up and deal with it." But I totally missed the point by rolling my eyes and saying, "Whatever!" before reading verses 35-36. He says that if we do all the things He's talking about in the preceding verses, then we

> *...will truly be acting as children of the Most High, for he is kind to the unthankful and to those who are wicked. You must be compassionate, just as your Father is compassionate* (The Book).

Many verses in the Bible refer to us as God's children. We talk about what a powerful example Christ's love for us is and how grateful we are in how He deals with us. We recognize the need to let His love and mercy flow through us as we raise our kids. Think about when we're watching one of our kids struggle with something that's really difficult, something bigger than they should be dealing with on their own, and how we want so badly to help. We want them to come to us and pour out their hearts so we can love on them, comfort them, and guide them through. God feels that way about us! *We* are *His* kids!

> *Jesus said, "Come to me, all of you who are weary and carry heavy burdens, and I will give you rest. Take my yoke upon you. Let me teach you, because I am humble and gentle at heart, and*

you will find rest for your souls. For my yoke is easy to bear, and the burden I give you is light" (Matthew 11:28-30, NLT).

God wants to be there for us. Yes, He wants us to call out to Him when times are tough. But more than that, He wants a relationship with us! The more we talk to Him, the more we recognize His voice when He speaks to us. We all have people in our life that we don't need Caller Id for. We know who they are as soon as they start speaking because we recognize their voice. God wants us to know His voice that well.

Jesus told us, "I command you to love each other in the same way that I love you" (John 15:12, The Book).

We're reminded to, "Be kind and compassionate to one another, forgiving each other, just as in Christ God forgave you" (Ephesians 4:32, NIV).

Wait a minute—I'm supposed to extend the same amount of grace to certain people that Christ gave me? That's a pretty tall order! I look at that and I think, "God, there's no way! I simply don't have that amount of love and compassion in me to really even consider such a thing!" God showed me that my thought process was based on a definition of myself that's no longer valid. It's who I used to be. He began showing me different things about who I am *now* that dispel that image. At the end of it, I can honestly say that while I may not have much compassion on my own, *He* is definitely building it in me.

My God will supply all your needs according to His riches in glory in Christ Jesus (Philippians 4:19, NASB).

Whenever I look at a situation that I know beyond a shadow of a doubt that He's been part of, the enormity and depth of His involvement blows me away! There's often no reason for the outcome other than God orchestrated it. One of the things I love about Jesus is that He knows the deeper need.

A man with leprosy came and knelt in front of Jesus, begging to be healed. "If you are willing, you can heal me and make me clean," he said. Moved with compassion, Jesus reached out and touched him. "I am willing," he said. "Be healed!" (Mark 1:40-41, NLT)

You have to consider the full circumstance that this man lived in. Once he was identified as having leprosy, he would've been forced to leave his wife, his kids, everything he took for granted as being part of his life, and had to live in a leper colony. Whenever lepers moved about in "normal" society, they had to constantly shout "Unclean! Unclean!" so others wouldn't touch them and possibly contract the disease themselves. Put yourself in this man's shoes for a moment. He can't hold his wife, he can't hug his kids, he can't spend time hanging out with his friends anymore because He's "unclean." Most likely he lost whatever vocation he had and was getting by the best way he could. That would be so hard!

During one of our cross-country moves, my wife and I were separated for a couple of months. I stayed in Louisiana wrapping things up, and she stayed with family in coastal Virginia getting the lay of the land, figuring out where we would live, and so on. Right around the three-week mark, I realized that I wanted a hug. I mean, I was craving a hug! It was a basic thing to want, but I deeply missed the simple intimacy of hugging my wife.

Let's go back to this man with leprosy. We don't know how long he'd had the disease, but He was desperate enough to come before Jesus and *beg* to be healed. What amazes me is that Jesus reached out and *touched* him. Can you imagine the impact of that touch on this man's heart? All he's asking for is to be healed, to be made whole, yet Jesus sees the deeper desire—to experience the loving touch of another human—and meets him there too.

Jesus didn't just heal him of leprosy; He gave that man his life back. I'm sure he went home and loved his family differently, he worshipped differently, and he cared for others differently. As followers of Christ, we've been restored and are recipients of God's love and grace. But are we extending the same love and grace Christ gave us to our families?

My youngest did something dumb one day, and I jumped on his case over it. Nothing was broken, life and limb were not at risk, yet I was gruff with him when I didn't need to be. I failed to treat him with compassion and mercy. I'm not advocating for weakness and an overabundance of sensitivity here, but as I assess my heart attitude in that situation, I have to admit that there was too much of me and not enough of Christ in my response. I failed to extend what I have been so freely given.

We need to examine ourselves and make sure that we're loving our wife, kids, those He has put in our life, the way they need to be loved. If I'm to be honest, I don't always do a good job of that. Why? That's not the example provided for us. Jesus could've healed the leper and sent him on his way. Instead, Jesus *touched* him and, in that moment, that man felt His love and was forever changed.

Discussion Questions

1. In what ways are we like the leper?

2. How does realizing what you've been forgiven of drive the way you treat others?

3. Will you extend His love, mercy, and grace to your kids? To your wife? To that annoying coworker?

✦40✦

1 Corinthians 9:25-27

The lyrics to Jesus Culture's song "Set a Fire" are simple but very powerful. I pray that those aren't just words that we sing, but that it's our heart's cry for Jesus to become a raging, purifying fire within that consumes us. Those words should reflect the depth of what Jesus means to us and reflect His refining work in our lives so that His kingdom, will, and purpose for our lives becomes our reality.

Jesus told us that we can't serve two masters, that we'll love one and hate the other. We say we're doing things to pursue Christ, but are we actively engaged or just going through the motions? What are we giving up to make room for Him? We say we understand that we'll never be perfect or free of sin while on this earth, but have we accepted that fact with an "It is what it is" attitude? Our level of dissatisfaction with who we are, with where we're at, and with what we're currently doing, should be growing in intensity. This should be spurring us on to become stronger, to have increased endurance where we don't have much and to have new victories in the weak and broken areas of our life.

The Apostle Paul said,

All athletes are disciplined in their training. They do it to win a prize that will fade away, but we do it for an eternal prize. So I run with purpose in every step. I am not just shadowboxing. I discipline my body like an athlete, training it to do what it should (1 Corinthians 9:25-27, NLT).

There's a correlation between what we put our time and effort into and who we are. If I start running, then I'll start losing weight, and eventually, I'll be able to run farther and faster. If I lift weights, then there should be some muscle development, and my clothes will fit differently. The point is that you'll be able to see the results of my efforts. It's not just about what we're doing; it's *how* we're doing it that makes the difference. If we don't train smart, wear good running shoes, or use good form when lifting something, we'll be setting ourselves up for an injury. *How* we go about disciplining and training ourselves matters a great deal because ultimately, it determines whether or not we reach our goal.

Think about how a boxer trains. They start out learning to throw a punch. Then they learn to throw another one. Then they put those two punches together. Additional punches, combinations, head movement, footwork, defensive maneuvers, along with strength and endurance training are added to their routines. They learn to study their opponent, to see rhythms and patterns in movement, to anticipate openings in a defense and to strike at the right time. Boxers spend their entire career learning to fight, and they're never done learning.

Just as boxers increase their skills, mental toughness, and understanding of individual combat, so must we continue to improve in our spiritual lives. We have to constantly be leaning forward. Reading the Bible, Christian books, and a commentary are good things, but what are we doing with them? All of that study should amount to something. What results are being made manifest in our lives because of our relationship with Jesus Christ? There has to progress.

> *Love the Lord your God with **all** your heart and with **all** your soul and with **all** your strength* (Deuteronomy 6:5, NIV, emphasis mine)

"All." This isn't attained overnight. It's something we work on our entire lives.

In the leadership schools I went to while in the military, they only celebrated the #1 ranked person in the class. The thought process was that a second place winner is really just a first place loser. That person got so close to being number one, so close to tasting victory, yet they failed. Perhaps that sounds a little harsh, but that's the culture. To be honest, I think that mentality applies here. We're not in competition with each other, but are we serving Christ or not? Are we putting in all that we have, or are we putting in what we feel like like doing? Albert Einstein famously said, "If you always do what you always did, you will always get what you always got."

As we continue to walk with Christ, our self-image changes from one tainted with pride to one recognizing our flaws and shortcomings in the stark light of His holiness. Who we are changes based on the things He says to us—about us. God has set aside specific tasks that He wants you and me to do. There are things that only *you* are supposed to accomplish. Kingdom things are being birthed inside each and every one of us. We need to ask God what steps we should be taking in order to attain them. Then, we need to be obedient and do as He says. We also need to measure things we're being told by others against what we *know* He's placed in our heart. We must protect the vision He has given us.

I was talking with a fellow believer at work one day about some things that were going on in the workplace and in life. He was very encouraging and started talking about a different career path that could lead to greater opportunities for me. His speech was flattering, but the direction he suggested didn't feel right. Now, he's a godly man and has great intentions, but the things he was talking about didn't line up with what I feel God has for me. I was telling my wife about the conversation later on, and I had barely finished recounting it, and she started telling me that this wasn't something I should do and why. Confirmation of God's purpose and plan from my wife is a beautiful and powerful thing.

There are things that each one of us is divinely created, refined, and positioned for. Will we accept *whatever* it is? It may be a life out on the mission field leading thousands to Christ. Maybe you're supposed to be a godly man in your house showing your wife, your kids, your siblings, and perhaps even your parents what a life submitted to Christ looks like. Maybe... Well, truly, it doesn't matter what it is. If God is asking you to do something, will you do it?

We have to be able to honestly assess ourselves. We cannot look at, or point at, anyone else and blame them for holding us back. We're responsible for who we are, for what we've done, and for our motives behind those things when we stand before the throne of God.

How are you different today compared to last year? Last month? Last week? Yesterday? If we truly are seeking His face (2 Chronicles 7:14), then there should be noticeable, measurable change because He's constantly speaking to us and guiding us.

Going back to Paul's analogy of an athlete in training, there's never really a day off. Athletes that are preparing for a competitive event may have a day of rest, but they don't kick back, eat cake, and watch TV all day. They're still focused on their diet, and they still do something to keep themselves moving. The enemy of our soul doesn't take time off, which means that we don't have time off either. We cannot afford to get spiritually lazy. We must stay focused and engaged.

Discussion Questions

1. Where do you spend the bulk of your time, energy, and focus?
2. What changes are your wife, kids, and those closest to you seeing compared to last week? Last month? Last year?
3. What areas of your life are you giving God more control of?

✢41✢

Deuteronomy 20:16-18

As the Israelites prepared to occupy the Promised Land, God instructed them,

> *For in the cities within the boundaries of the Promised Land you are to save no one; destroy every living thing. Utterly destroy the Hittites, the Amorites, the Canaanites, the Perizzites, the Hivites, and the Jebusites. This is the commandment of the Lord your God. The purpose of this command is to prevent the people of the land from luring you into idol worship and into participation in their loathsome customs, thus sinning deeply against the Lord your God* (Deuteronomy 20:16-18, TLB).

Each city had its own king, its own army, and its own defense systems. The land that's "flowing with milk and honey" *was* there, but they had to conquer it. In order to obtain the Promised Land, the Israelites had to eliminate the evil that had taken up residence. So it is with us.

> *Jesus told His disciples, "Whoever wants to be my disciple must deny themselves and take up their cross and follow me"* (Matthew 16:24, NIV).

In this instance "deny" means to disown, reject, renounce, abandon, or to turn one's back on.[1] In other words, we need to be about the business of eliminating the evil in our lives while we're pursuing Jesus Christ. Action is required! Holiness and righteousness aren't going to come down like manna. In order to obtain them, we have to put to death the things we used to embrace.

> *Submit yourselves, then, to God. Resist the devil, and he will flee from you* (James 4:7, NIV).

We have to come to a place where we know that we can't do "this" on our own. Whatever "this" happens to be at that moment, we have to acknowledge that we need God in order to successfully resist the devil. Then we're able to move forward with Christ. This principle never ceases to be true. We all have areas of life where we're weak and susceptible to temptation. The only way to conquer them is to admit that on our own we can't defeat them. Otherwise, we would've already done so, and these things wouldn't still be part of our life.

For we are not fighting against flesh-and-blood enemies, but against evil rulers and authorities of the unseen world, against mighty powers in this dark world, and against evil spirits in the heavenly places (Ephesians 6:12, NLT).

There are certain things in life that just don't make sense. Some of the evil things people do defy normal, rational, and civilized thought processes. The only explanation that makes sense is that there's an evil force exerting its authority and power in those situations. We give Satan authority in our lives when we start agreeing with a thought or temptation he's put before us.

Each person is tempted when they are dragged away by their own evil desire and enticed. Then, after desire has conceived, it gives birth to sin; and sin, when it is full-grown, gives birth to death (James 1:14-15, NIV).

*Jesus says, "I have given you authority over **all** the power of the enemy"* (Luke 10:19, NLT, emphasis mine).

He also said, "You can ask for anything in my name, and I will do it, so that the Son can bring glory to the Father" (John 14:13, NLT).

Through Jesus, we will, not can, we *will* have victory in our life. However, it takes effort. If we want to move beyond where we are now, we have to purposefully engage the things that are in our way and eliminate them. We have to shift our mentality from a defensive one (Lord, please keep me from booze/drugs/porn/materialism) to an offensive one. (I bind you in Jesus' name, and I command you to get out!)

> *No temptation has overtaken you except what is common to mankind. And God is faithful: he will not let you be tempted beyond what you can bear. But when you are tempted, he will also provide a way out so that you can endure it* (1 Corinthians 10:13, NIV).

Remember, God is always with us and always provides an "out" in every situation. We need to look for it and take it. Adopting an offensive mentality in our spiritual life makes a tremendous difference in how we approach our walk, how we pray, and how we go about accomplishing our kingdom purpose.

I don't want to foster a loose or reckless mentality here. We will only win our battles if we're aligned with Christ and operating within His authority and His will. It is only through the power of Jesus Christ that we should engage the things in our life that don't belong. If we try on our own, we *will* lose.

I'm reminded of Acts 19:11-17 where seven sons of a leading priest tried casting out an evil spirit from a man saying, "I command you in the name of Jesus, whom Paul preaches, to come out!" (NLT) They didn't have a personal relationship with Jesus and weren't operating within His authority or will. As a result, all seven of the brothers were severely beaten by the demon possessed man. We need not be afraid, but we should not be dismissive of our enemy either.

We need to understand that we're being watched as we move forward, not just by our family or our co-workers but by the enemy of our soul. Christine Caine once said, "Whenever you are taking new ground, the enemy will forge a weapon to try to stop you." There's an immediacy in that response. It's not enough to sit back and think, "Well, the enemy is a defeated foe. Jesus has already defeated sin and death." Satan is not going to give up easily. Every inch of ground we take in Jesus' name will be contested. We need to own our role in this life and live it with the full knowledge that Satan wants to eliminate us. We *must* fight our battles in Jesus' name, and through Him, we will win.

Discussion Questions

1. What does it mean to you that we have authority over all the powers of our enemy?

2. How does that impact the way you approach things you're struggling with?

3. How do you view this life differently, knowing that we're living in a spiritual battlefield?

[1]Strong's Concordance, Greek—533

⇢42⇠

Isaiah 48:17

Like it or not, as parents, we pass parts of our brokenness on to our kids. Granted, they have their own issues and make their own choices in life, but by our actions, we are demonstrating what is acceptable. I can't exactly discipline my kids for banging stuff around and breaking things when they're angry if that's what they see me doing. We have to demonstrate the values and principles we expect them to adhere to. How we speak to and treat our wife and our kids help frame the person they see themselves to be in the future. We are to show God's love, mercy, compassion, and forgiveness in our home. *We* are! Are we doing that?

*God says, "I am the Lord your God, who teaches **you** what is best for you, who directs **you** in the way you should go"* (Isaiah 48:17, NIV, emphasis mine).

Life is hard, and there's no user manual that we can search through to help us navigate most of the stuff we face. Unless I allow God to refine me and lead me forward, I'll follow familiar thought processes and behavior patterns that are tragically flawed. I've come to the realization that I *don't* know what's best for me, but He does! It's only through His work in my heart and in my life that I can change and raise my kids in a way that pleases His heart.

For some of us, our kids are already grown and out on their own. However, you are *still* setting the example for them. What is your life giving them permission to do? For those of us with kids still living at home, are we loving them and giving them grace when needed? Notice that I didn't say "deserved." Grace is bestowed as it is needed. Are we showing compassion as we discipline them, or are we assigning consequences in a detached, clinical, manner? (You did "this," the outcome was "that," and here's what you've earned. Buh-bye.) Are we praying over our kids as if their life hangs in the balance? I can assure you, it does.

Train up a child in the way he should go: and when he is old, he will not depart from it (Proverbs 22:6, KJV).

The last part of James 5:16 tells us that,

The earnest prayer of a righteous person has great power and produces wonderful results (NLT).

One of the things I've come to know is that I'm here today because my parents constantly prayed over me. There have been several situations in life where I could have been killed. I look back and I *know* that God intervened and kept me alive and safe. My parents set aside time every day to read the Bible and cover each and every one of us in prayer. I feel it and am blessed by it. They're quick to admit that they're not perfect, but I can assure you that they continue to lean forward into being the person they're supposed to be. I can see it in their lives. Even though I'm an adult with a family of my own, my parents are still leading me, still showing me the way forward.

It's all great and wonderful to sit here and talk about what we should be doing and where our focus should be, but the truth is that when the pressure of life is on, these can be very tough principles to adhere to. It is guaranteed that even attempting to do things differently than we've always done them will cost you a fair amount of pride and will push you out into deep water that you're not prepared to be in. I wish I could tell you that the journey gets easier, but it doesn't. Your sinful nature will always be screaming as it's subjected to His will. However, choosing to be obedient does get easier. We'll start seeing different outcomes the more we trust the Holy Spirit's leading and step out into the unknown of doing things His way. It doesn't take long to understand that we can't do this without God.

But seek ye first the kingdom of God, and his righteousness; and all these things shall be added unto you (Matthew 6:33, KJV).

Paul reminds us that,

Do you not know that your bodies are temples of the Holy Spirit, who is in you, whom you have received from God? You are not your own (1 Corinthians 6:19, NIV).

We must never forget that we represent God the Father in our home. We can't force people to love God and serve Him. But we can show them what a life submitted to Christ looks like. We must demonstrate the same level of love, compassion, forgiveness, and mercy we want from God to those closest to us. Talk is cheap. We can't give lip service to God and not demonstrate real, heart level, change. There must be tangible change and progress in who we are. It is impossible to have a relationship with Jesus Christ and not be changed. So, where is that change? Is your wife seeing it? Are your kids experiencing it?

Discussion Questions

1. What is your life giving the people around you permission to do?

2. What's a recent example from your life where you chose God's will over yours?

3. Are we giving the same level of love, compassion, and forgiveness that we've received?

⇥43⇤

Three Stones

All who listen to my instructions and follow them are wise, like a man who builds his house on solid rock. Though the rain comes in torrents, and the floods rise and the storm winds beat against his house, it won't collapse, for it is built on rock. But those who hear my instructions and ignore them are foolish, like a man who builds his house on sand. For when the rains and floods come, and storm winds beat against his house, it will fall with a mighty crash (Matthew 7:24-27, TLB).

We're *guaranteed* to face storms in this life but on what is your foundation built—firm bedrock or soft soil? I want to briefly examine three stones referenced in the Bible and see what we can learn from them.

The first stone is Jesus Christ.

This is what the Almighty Lord says: "I am going to lay a rock in Zion, a rock that has been tested, a precious cornerstone, a solid foundation. Whoever believes in him will not worry" (Isaiah 28:16, GW).

In order to understand the significance of Jesus being *the* cornerstone, we have to first understand why a cornerstone is important. In modern construction, the cornerstone is largely ceremonial. It's generally a different type of stone that is clearly distinguishable. You'll frequently see the building name, a government or organizational seal, and the date the building was commissioned on it. However, in traditional construction methods, the cornerstone is the first and most significant stone laid. The cornerstone was usually larger, set deeper, and was a higher quality of stone as it is vital in supporting the rest of the structure. The placement of this stone establishes the location of the building, and the adjoining foundation stones are set in reference to this stone.

Jesus reminded the leading priests and Pharisees of Psalms 118:22-23 saying,

> *The stone rejected by the builders has now become the cornerstone. This is the Lord's doing, and it is marvelous to see* (Matthew 21:42, The Book).

Jesus is *our* cornerstone. He's our firm foundation. He orients us and provides support. He is what we hold onto when everything around us is unstable. He is our shelter during the storms of life.

The second stone is the foundation stones of Jericho.

Joshua 6 tells the story of Jericho's fall. God tells Joshua that He has given them the city, its king, and its army. Everything and everybody were to be destroyed as a sacrifice to the Lord. The only things permitted to be removed were things made from gold, silver, bronze, or iron, set apart as sacred and were to be brought to the Lord's treasury. Once the city was destroyed, Joshua declared,

> *May the curse of the Lord fall on anyone who tries to rebuild the city of Jericho. At the cost of his firstborn son, he will lay its foundation. At the cost of his youngest son, he will set up its gates* (Joshua 6:26, The Book).

In 1 Kings we're told that

> *A man from Bethel rebuilt Jericho. When he laid the foundations, his oldest son, Abiram died. And when he finally completed it by setting up the gates, his youngest son, Segub died. This all happened according to the message from the Lord concerning Jericho spoken by Joshua son of Nun* (1 Kings 16:34, The Book).

The city of Jericho was built in an extremely desirable location.

It was a key city to the entire region as it sat near a major trade route. Even today it's an attractive place to live with an average temperature of 71-72 degrees, freshwater springs, and fertile soil.

God Himself destroyed the walls of Jericho, and He declared that the entire city, its inhabitants, and their possessions, down to the animals, should be destroyed. Through Joshua, He declared that the city should never be rebuilt and a high price would be paid should it be attempted. Even though quite a few centuries had passed, when His warning was disregarded, the price had to be paid.

If God has destroyed something, there's never a reason to go back and try to rebuild any part of it. Things He has saved us from and told us should be off limits, should be put behind us. If we try to rebuild those former strongholds, we will indeed pay the price.

The third stone is us.

Come to Christ, who is the living cornerstone of God's temple. He was rejected by the people, but he is precious to God who chose him. And now God is building you, as living stones, into his spiritual temple (1 Peter 2:4-5, The Book).

We are "living stones" being built into God's spiritual temple. It's only when I started thinking about some of the ancient structures that the enormity of this started to settle into me. Consider things such as the Great Pyramids in Egypt, Machu Picchu in Peru, or Angor Wat in Cambodia. Each of these places is constructed with gigantic stones that were quarried and fit together so tightly that even now, a piece of paper cannot be inserted between them. Each stone was purposefully selected and shaped to fit in a specific spot within the overall structure, then placed with such intentionality and precision that it rivals modern engineering. Truly, these are magnificent structures, and they inspire awe on many levels.

The stones used at those ancient sites had to be quarried,

shaped, refined, and put in place. *We* were identified by Christ, brought out from the depths of sin that we used to inhabit, and are continually being refined and positioned where God has us to be. As the Master Builder, He intimately knows our strengths and weaknesses. He intentionally shapes and positions us, as well as those around us, so that there's no way for the enemy to find and exploit a gap between us. He satisfies the desires of our heart even though we may not know what they are. *We* are magnificent stones that have been purposely chosen, refined, and placed by the Lord our God.

We are part of the Kingdom of God in more ways than we realize. Our every motive, thought, and deed must be aligned with Him. His ways are not our ways, and we are not our own. We've been bought with a high price. We're constantly being refined and positioned according to *His* master plan, and it is indeed a beautiful thing! God has removed things from each of our lives. He's torn down what we built and the person we made ourselves to be, and has told us to never go there again. With Christ as our cornerstone, our solid foundation, we are individually designed and refined for a specific purpose within His Kingdom!

Discussion Questions

1. How is Jesus the cornerstone in your life?

2. What is God working on removing or tearing down in your life?

3. In what ways is He refining and shaping you?

→44←

Purpose

I've been reading a book written by retired Admiral William McRaven, who served as a SEAL and commanded special operations forces at the highest level. In his book, McRaven lists six principles of special operations warfare and examines specific combat actions conducted by special operations forces. Of the principles put forth, "Purpose" has held my attention throughout the book. Purpose is noted as being a moral factor, and McRaven states that,

> Purpose is understanding and then executing the prime objective of the mission regardless of emerging obstacles or opportunities (that might distract you from the primary objective). There are two aspects of this principle. First, the purpose must be clearly defined by the mission statement: rescue the POWs, destroy the dry dock, sink the battleship, etc. The second aspect...is personal commitment... and the men must be inspired with a sense of personal dedication that knows no limitations."[1]

At the conclusion of one particular case study he says,

> Understanding the purpose of the mission and being committed to fulfilling that purpose is essential to success.[2]

I enjoy reading these kinds of books, and honestly, I see a lot of crossover between the mentality of those engaged in combat and what our mindset should be regarding our spiritual journey. A guy I know was describing some of the incredibly difficult situations he faced during a combat tour in Iraq and said, "All I knew was that I was going home, and that other guy—wasn't." For him, it was just that simple. I'm going to survive; I'm going home to *my* family so I can love and care for them; I'm going to continue moving forward, and I will eliminate whatever obstacle is in my way. *Nothing* will prevent me from attaining this goal.

Why don't we think like this in our spiritual lives? Why is it that the bag of chips, the bottle of soda or alcohol, the computer, the slot machines, etc. have more power in our lives than Jesus Christ? Part of it is we've not claimed ownership of our purpose. We've not steeled our minds and set our focus on completing the mission He's given to us.

Stand steady, and don't be afraid of suffering for the Lord (1 Timothy 4:5, TLB).

Not everything is going to be easy. Some of it is just going to be hard, and there are things that are ours to do. No one else can do these things for us. However, we should not attempt to do them without Him.

Bring others to Christ. Leave nothing undone that you ought to do. I have fought long and hard for my Lord, and through it all I have kept true to him (1 Timothy 4:7, TLB).

James 4:17 puts it rather plainly,

"Whoever knows what is right but doesn't do it is sinning" (GW).

One of the key components to the success of the operations studied in the book is overall training and specific mission rehearsals. The men were made to be in top physical condition and were kept that way. Their familiarity and proficiency with weapons, explosives, as well as the equipment they would be using was honed. They conducted mission specific rehearsals as often, and as thoroughly, as possible so that when they were in actual combat, they reacted instinctively and moved towards their target(s). It should be no different with us.

Jesus says, *"No one can serve two masters. Either you will hate the one and love the other, or you will be devoted to the one and despise the other"* (Matthew 6:24, NIV).

Submit yourselves, then, to God. Resist the devil, and he will flee from you (James 4:7, NIV).

We have to be committed. We have to dedicate ourselves to doing what we ought to be doing. This is all great but what does this have to do with purpose? For that answer, let's look to Jesus.

The Spirit of the Sovereign Lord is upon me, for the Lord has anointed me to bring good news to the poor. He has sent me to comfort the brokenhearted and to proclaim that captives will be released and prisoners will be freed. He has sent me to tell those who mourn that the time of the Lord's favor has come, and with it, the day of God's anger against their enemies (Isaiah 61:1-2, NLT).

The Son of Man did not come to be served, but to serve, and to give his life as a ransom for many (Matthew 20:28, NIV).

Healthy people don't need a doctor—sick people do. I have come to call not those who think they are righteous, but those who know they are sinners (Mark 2:17, NLT, emphasis mine).

For the Son of Man came to seek and save those who are lost (Luke 19:10, NLT).

For I have come down from heaven to do the will of God who sent me, not to do my own will (John 6:38, NLT).

I was reading in Mark where Jesus started telling the disciples that they were going to Jerusalem, and He would be betrayed and killed there. Mark 10:32 describes the overall mood during their journey.

They were now on the way to Jerusalem, and Jesus was walking ahead of them. The disciples were filled with dread and the people following behind were overwhelmed with fear. Taking the twelve disciples aside, Jesus once more began to describe everything that was about to happen to him in Jerusalem (The Book).

I find it interesting that those following Jesus were filled with fear and dread. Jesus was resolute even though He understood what lay ahead. He wasn't confused about why He came to earth as a man. He kept the mission in front of Himself and in front of His disciples. Jesus rebuked Peter when he suggested that maybe Jesus didn't need to die. He deliberately left an area when the crowds around Him began wanting to make Him an earthly king. He knew what He had to do and was committed to seeing it through. *Nothing* was going to prevent Him from achieving His purpose here on earth.

We too must keep God's purpose for our lives in front of us. We must train ourselves to stay within His will and plan for our lives. We have to want to complete the task at hand regardless of what it might cost us. I don't mean "want" like I want to lose 20 lbs but do little to make it happen. I'm talking about being at the bottom of the pool and wanting air. We need to have an all-consuming desire to achieve and attain what God has for us that is at such an intensity level and depth within us that it becomes ingrained into our lives—an inseparable part of who we are.

We have to believe in, and be fully committed to, what we're doing. Our proficiency comes through studying His Word and *applying* it in our lives. We have to seek His face and constantly be listening for His voice as He leads and guides us. We have to keep our eyes focused on the cross, and in doing so, we'll be able to move *through* whatever obstacles present themselves.

I'm reminded of the lyrics to an old hymn, "Turn your eyes upon Jesus. Look full in His wonderful face, and the things of earth will grow strangely dim in the light of His glory and grace." If we stay focused on what's important to God's heart, we cannot fail. We may stumble, but we will not fall. But we have to be fully committed to fulfilling His will and purpose in our lives. It is only then that we'll be able to achieve success in the ways that matter for eternity.

Discussion Questions

1. How are you applying what God shows you during your devotional time or during men's group meetings?

2. What kingdom purpose do you identify with as being your own?

3. What's an example of something that's "yours" to do but have not asked for or accepted His help with?

---

[1] William McRaven, *Spec Ops: Case Studies in Special Operations Warfare: Theory and Practice,* (New York, Presido Press, 1996), pp 21-23.

[2] Ibid., p 283.

→45←

Isaiah 8:11

I've been going through the wringer for quite a while now. The things I've been walking through have been hugely refining and tiring. I do see the why in most of it, which is an incredible gift to be given, but there are times when I just feel worn out. The thing is, we all get tired at some point and begin thinking, *Lord, why?*

We have to recognize that if we're leaning forward in our faith, we're going to meet resistance. We're going to get tired. We're going to stumble. It's in those moments that we get a look at who we really are and just how much of our life we've turned over to Jesus Christ. For me, it's been a little surprising at what comes out when I'm being squeezed. No matter how hard we try, our best efforts simply aren't going to be enough. The attacks are going to come. Thankfully, we're able to turn to Jesus for strength and protection.

At the end of World War I, France decided that they needed a strong defensive line against Germany, so using lessons learned from that war, they constructed what became known as the Maginot Line. Although they were most heavily fortified on the borders of Switzerland, Germany, and Luxembourg, the defensive line stretched across the western border of France. The French neglected to heavily fortify the historical invasion route taken by Germany through Belgium, choosing instead to show respect for the declared neutrality of Belgium. They did, however, draw up contingency plans to reinforce positions along what was an obvious invasion route.

The Ardennes region of France was thought to be an unlikely invasion route because of the rough terrain, thick forests, and ridges. There were some defensive posts built but nothing too extensive. The plan was to delay any invasion force that might try to come through while additional forces were mobilized for a counterattack. Germany saw the defensive gap in Belgium and made note of the weaker defensive positions through the Ardennes forest and violently attacked through both of them, gaining control of France. Germany did not care about Belgium's declaration of neutrality or that the route through the Ardennes would be difficult. They only cared about occupying France, and they took the necessary steps to obtain that goal.

In Matthew 10:16 Jesus likened Satan and his followers to wolves. Wolves are very intelligent and patient hunters. They're known to observe their prey in a casual manner, but what they're really doing is looking for an opportunity to kill that animal and devour it. Jesus made that correlation intentionally.

Satan is an intelligent being, as are the other fallen angels. They do not want us to attain what God has for us or to achieve what we're capable of in our spiritual lives. The enemy of our soul watches us carefully and strikes with the intent of killing us. So we can't kick back, think we've got it covered, and keep doing the same things spiritually and think it's going to be enough.

Luke 4:1-13 tells us that during Jesus' time of fasting in the wilderness, Satan tempted Him for those 40 days. At the end of it, "he left him until the next opportunity came" (The Book). Jesus didn't have it easy after those 40 days. In Hebrews 2:10 we're told that Christ was made perfect through His suffering. Satan knew who Jesus was and undoubtedly took every opportunity to attack Him. If *Jesus* made time to go off and pray, deliberately spending time communicating and aligning Himself with the Father, how much more do we need to do that? We must put the time into our relationship with God and allow Him to have greater influence in our lives.

During my devotional time, often something will jump out at

me so I'll write down the scripture reference and a brief note with what I'm thinking at that moment. Individually, these scriptures mean something to me, but recently I combined them all, like a statement, and they speak a very strong message. So, I'm going to read them, in the order they were shown to me, providing the references at the end.

- The Lord has said to me in the strongest terms: "Do not think like everyone else does."
- "Stop loving this evil world and all that it offers you, for when you love the world, you show that you do not have the love of the Father in you."
- "The world would love you if you belonged to it, but you don't... The people of this world will hate you because you belong to me."
- "Let heaven fill your thoughts. Do not think only about things down here on earth. For you died when Christ died, and your real life is hidden with Christ in God."

(Isaiah 8:11; 1 John 2:15; John 15:19,21; Colossians 3:2-3; The Book).

Jesus isn't standing at the edge of the path of righteousness, trying to get our attention calling, "Yoohoo! Ummm...fellas?" He's not engaged in a spiritual version of Red Rover. He came to seek and save the lost *here* on earth, and He did it as a human. He came to us! He overcame every temptation, defeated sin and death, then left the grave behind Him. There is *no other* source of love, or strength, or life, or freedom that can compare to what He offers.

I know that there's still entirely too much of me evident in my life, and it's probably the same for you. In the wide world of options, we have exactly two—we can quit, or we can continue forward. Not much of an option set really, but there they are. Life can be a real grind at times, but are we allowing God to use that to refine us and draw us closer or are we just getting worn down?

Turn your burdens over to the Lord, and he will take care of you (Psalm 55:22, GW).

The full might and power of who He is, is *always* available to us. Always! All we have to do is reach out. Mother Teresa famously said, "Yesterday is gone. Tomorrow has not yet come. We have only today. Let us begin." I love that. What we did yesterday was great, but what is God doing today? Where is He wanting to lead us today? What is He saying to us today? We cannot keep looking backwards and think that what we've done is going to be enough. Satan is looking for a gap, a weak area in our lives, that he can attack and exploit. We *must* keep moving forward in Christ.

Discussion Questions

1. What areas of weakness or spiritual gaps have you left open for the enemy to identify and exploit?

2. How do you keep moving forward in Christ when you are feeling worn down?

3. What does "turn your burdens over to the Lord" mean to you? What does that look like?

⇢46⇠

Not a Hoof Shall Be Left Behind

During Moses and Pharaoh's initial conversation about letting the Israelites go, Moses said,

> *This is what the Lord God of Israel says: "Let my people go into the desert to celebrate a festival in my honor." Pharaoh asked, "Who is the Lord? Why should I obey him and let Israel go? I don't know the Lord, and I won't let Israel go." They (Moses and Aaron) replied, "The God of the Hebrews has met with us. Please let us travel three days into the desert to offer sacrifices to the Lord our God"* (Exodus 5:1-3, GW).

Pharaoh did not relent but after nine plagues ravaged the land, we're told that,

> *Pharaoh called for Moses and said, "Go and worship Jehovah—but let your flocks and herds stay here; you can even take your children with you." "No," Moses said, "we must take our flocks and herds for sacrifices and burnt offerings to Jehovah our God. Not a hoof shall be left behind; for we must have sacrifices for the Lord our God, and we do not know what he will choose until we get there"* (Exodus 10:24-26, TLB).

That seems like an odd condition doesn't it? "Y'all can go ahead but leave the animals here." It's interesting that the Israelites were free to go as long as they did not bring the very things required for a sacrifice. I love Moses' firm response, "No...not a hoof shall be left behind."

The first chapter of Job tells the story of a godly man who made a regular practice of offering a sacrifice for each of his children. Job would purify each child and offer sacrifices in atonement for them. When God gave Satan permission to test Job, the very first thing Satan attacked was Job's oxen, donkeys, sheep, and camels. His ability to offer a sacrifice was eliminated.

While we no longer have the blood requirement from the Law of Moses because of what Jesus accomplished on the cross, God still requires that a sacrifice be made.

> *Beloved friends, what should be our proper response to God's marvelous mercies? I encourage you to surrender yourselves to God to be his sacred, living sacrifices. And live in holiness, experiencing all that delights his heart* (Romans 12:1, TPT).

> *Put to death therefore what is earthly in you* (Colossians 3:5, ESV).

> *Love the Lord your God with all your heart and with all your soul and with all your strength* (Deuteronomy 6:5, NIV).

> *But seek ye first the kingdom of God, and his righteousness; and all these things shall be added unto you* (Matthew 6:33, KJV).

God requires *all* of who we are to be brought and dedicated to Him. We are to surrender our hearts, thoughts, and desires—who we see ourselves to be—to Christ. Often our greatest challenge is letting go of who we see ourselves to be. As we do, He is able to guide us away from the things we've done and who we've been. He is able to show us the things that matter to His heart and show us the person He sees us to be. As we offer ourselves to God, He is able to refine and purify us, making us holy.

Why should we care? Can't we just "keep on keepin' on" and still love Jesus? I mean, sacrificing things we've long held close in exchange for whatever God has for us is not an easy or comfortable process. I know that when God is working on something in me, I feel "off" in my spirit, and my wife assures me that I'm grumpier in general. So, why bother? Wouldn't I actually be doing my family a favor by hanging onto whatever it is that God is identifying and sparing them my grumpy mood? Uhhhh...no.

Let's go back to Job. God told Satan not to physically harm him, but that protection wasn't extended to his children. Remember how Job regularly purified and atoned for his kids? Right after Satan eliminated Job's ability to offer a sacrifice, all of his children were killed. Our level of submission to Jesus, the degree to which we offer ourselves as a sacrifice to God, has a direct impact on the spiritual covering we provide for our family. Satan isn't just looking to eliminate us; he wants everyone in our sphere of influence too. If we stop sacrificing the things God identifies as belonging to Him, we're no longer positioned to protect those who matter most to us.

We keep talking about sacrifice, and, if I'm to be honest, I struggle to get away from the ritualistic meaning of the word where an animal is slaughtered and presented as an offering. While this is definitely applicable, in order to gain a broader perspective, let's look at the great American pastime of baseball.

In baseball, there's such a thing known as a sacrifice fly where the batter hits the ball, it is caught by the opposing team, and a teammate of the batter advances and scores. The batter's official batting statistics are not negatively impacted (as if he'd struck out or if his hit had simply been caught). Instead, the batter is credited with a "run batted in," which is a good thing. On the downside, if the batter had a long hitting streak going (meaning he's been hitting the ball every time he has a turn at bat), a sacrifice fly ends that streak. While the team benefits from a sacrifice fly, the batter pays a price in their personal performance records.

Applied to our spiritual lives, our sacrifice isn't just about us—it's about advancing the Kingdom of God. Our sacrifice impacts so much more than we realize! If I sacrifice (completely give over to God) my presumed identity as someone who gets angry, then He's able to re-define me into someone who responds in love, addressing the heart issue being displayed. Having been subject to this refining process for some time now, I can testify to the difference God's way makes compared to my way. Sacrificing that aspect of who I thought I was to God allowed Him to show me who I really am. As a result, I'm able to have a greater impact on those around me.

For you died when Christ died, and your real life is hidden with Christ in God (Colossians 3:3, The Book).

As soon as I accepted Christ into my heart and my life, I was forgiven of everything I had done. I became a new creation and the old me ceased to exist (2 Corinthians 5:17). I still have to walk in that reality though. But how? I see myself a certain way and simply don't know *how* to be different. By laying all of who I am before God, I sacrifice (completely give over) myself to Him. It's then that God can start showing me who I am in Him. When I let go of whom I see me to be, I'm able to take on His truth, His reality.

"Not a hoof shall be left behind." Hold nothing back. Give it all to Him.

Discussion Questions

1. What does being a "living sacrifice" to God look like in your life?

2. What are you holding back or holding onto instead of surrendering it to Christ?

3. What impact would those closest to you see or feel if you sacrificed that area to God?

✦47✦

Prodigal Son

Luke 15:11-32 tells us the parable of the Prodigal Son. Verses 20-22 say,

And while he (the prodigal son) was still a long distance away, his father saw him coming. Filled with love and compassion, he ran to his son, embraced him, and kissed him. His son said to him, "Father, I have sinned against both heaven and you, and I am no longer worthy of being called your son." But his father said to the servants, "Quick! Bring the finest robe in the house and put it on him. Get a ring for his finger, and sandals for his feet. And kill the calf we have been fattening in the pen. We must celebrate with a feast, for this son of mine was dead and has now returned to life. He was lost, but now he is found." So the party began (The Book).

Now, after the son had squandered all the money his father had given him and was destitute, he decided to return home and plead for mercy from his father. He left the place where he was feeding pigs just to survive and had just walked a great distance. He was barefoot and probably smelled really bad. Yet his father ordered the finest robe in the house, a ring, and sandals be brought and put on his son.

Maybe it's just me, but I've always wondered what happened with the son after that. He still smelled bad, so did he take a bath or something before going to the feast? He still had consequences to walk out with his family, and he and his father still had to have discussions regarding how his restoration would come about, so when did they take place? Regardless of when he got cleaned up and when they had those difficult talks, I imagine that the son lived the rest of his life working hard for his father because he *knew* what he had and valued it in a way that he had not before.

I find the father's actions so powerful. He embraced and kissed his son despite the physical stench and the griminess of his appearance. He chose to forgo the hard discussions that needed to occur about the past, the present, and the future, and instead celebrated the return of his lost son and restored him. God does the same thing for us. Regardless of where we've been and what we've done, He keeps looking for us to come back to Him. When we do, He's right there to embrace us and welcome us home. He forgives us completely and begins the process of cleaning us up and showing us the way forward.

We can't keep looking back at what we used to do. There are times when I'm flooded with memories of the hurtful, stupid things I've done. They are somewhat paralyzing to look at, and it's a blatant attempt to chain me to the person I used to be. Satan would *love* to keep us in a place where we're busy looking at our past. If we're doing that, we're not exactly moving forward with power and authority in Jesus' name, are we?

Jesus Christ redeemed us, set us free, and put us on the path of righteousness. How can we move into all that God has planned for us to do if we're spending all of our time repenting for things that He's already forgiven us of? That just doesn't make sense.

> *For we are God's handiwork, created in Christ Jesus to do good works, which God prepared in advance for us to do* (Ephesians 2:10, NIV).

In his book, *Four Cups*, Chris Hodges says,

> God put you on planet Earth at this exact time and place so that you can fulfill the purpose for which you were created. ...God deliberately made you the way you are. He didn't create you and then think, *Hmmm, now what can I do*

with this one? ...God had something in mind for you to do and then he created you to do it.[1]

How do we know what we're supposed to be doing? How do we know if we're even on the right track or in the right place? If we're listening for His voice, God will guide us into our kingdom purpose. God gave each of us talents and abilities. As we give more and more of ourselves to Him, He's able to show us how to use our gifts for their intended purpose. The Bible promises us that if we seek His face, we will find Him, and He will always be with us. If we're truly looking to connect with and serve God, He will guide us into all that He has for us.

As part of teaching the disciples to pray, Jesus said, "Give us this day our daily bread" (Matthew 6:11, ESV). It occurs to me that He's not just offering us physical sustenance. Our wants and desires also get fed on a daily basis. To whom do we turn when they rise up, cry out, and demand to be fed? Notice that it's not "where" or "to what" do we turn, it's *to whom* do we turn.

God isn't the only one who prepares things that will satisfy our hunger. Satan regularly perverts what God has created and provided in an effort to entice us and lead us away. So, if there are tables prepared for us, and they all contain things that will feed our wants and desires, whose table will we partake of?

Thou preparest a table before me in the presence of mine enemies (Psalm 23:5, KJV).

Oh, taste and see that the LORD is good! (Psalm 34:8, ESV)

And this same God who takes care of me will supply all your needs from his glorious riches, which have been given to us in Christ Jesus (Philippians 4:19, NLT, emphasis mine).

Our heavenly Father is wise, loving, and will provide for our every want, desire, and need. He knows us best and loves us most; we only need to trust Him.

Discussion Questions

1. We've all been the Prodigal Son. What was it like for you to be embraced by the Father?

2. God has something for each of us to do. If you knew that you would never see the outcome of your obedience and faithfulness, would you still do what He's asking of you?

3. God created you for a specific purpose. How does that change your view of your role in this life?

[1] Chris Hodges, *Four Cups: God's Timeless Promises for a Life of Fulfillment* (Illinois, Tyndale Momentum, 2014), pp 47,79.

⊹48⊰

Isaiah 22:11-14

In chapter 22, Isaiah briefly relates the conditions, turmoil, and tragedy occurring within Jerusalem as it was being conquered. He talks about some of the steps taken to prepare for the siege and speaks to the emotion he feels seeing the destruction and suffering around him. But listen to what he says in verses 11-14,

> *But all your feverish plans are to no avail because you never ask God for help. He is the one who planned this long ago. The Lord, the Lord Almighty, called you to weep and mourn. He told you to shave your heads in sorrow for your sins and to wear clothes of sackcloth to show your remorse. But instead, you dance and play; you slaughter sacrificial animals, feast on meat, and drink wine. "Let's eat, drink, and be merry," you say. "What's the difference, for tomorrow we die." The Lord Almighty has revealed to me that this sin will **never** be forgiven until the day you die. That is the judgement of the Lord, the Lord Almighty* (The Book, emphasis mine).

In Amos 4 God lists all of the things He's brought against the nation of Israel to get their attention and cause them to turn back to Him. He brought hunger, ruined crops, withheld rain, sent blight and mildew as well as locusts, caused men to die in battle, and destroyed cities. Through all of this, God says to them, "Yet you wouldn't return to me" (v. 8, TLB). In verses 12-13 He declares,

> *Therefore, I will bring upon you all these further disasters I have announced. Prepare to meet your God as he comes in judgement, you people of Israel!* (The Book)

The people of Israel deliberately ignored God's call to repentance, and they blatantly forged ahead in their sin. They refused to consult Him as to what they should do and didn't turn to Him in times of trouble. All of this resulted in Israel being warned by God that He's coming, not to rescue them, but in judgment.

At this point, the Israelites had been hearing about the need to abandon their idolatry and return to worshipping the one, true God from different prophets for more than 100 years. They'd been hearing it for so long that they had hardened their hearts and continued doing what they wanted to do. As I read verses 12-13, I have to wonder if the Israelites really understood the weight of God's warning or the scope of what that would look like.

I heard the partial testimony of someone who'd been an enforcer in a motorcycle gang. He said that he was the guy you never wanted to see pull up to your house. Once he arrived, there was no turning back, and things were never again going to be the same for that person. The person receiving this visit would know who this guy was and why he was there without needing to be told. I imagine that the person being visited would be filled with dread and fear. No amount of begging or pleading would likely dissuade the enforcer from delivering the full "message" with which he'd been sent. As I picture all of this, the two words that most readily come to mind are "brutal" and "unrelenting."

With that example in mind, think about "the Lord, the Lord Almighty" telling you in no uncertain terms that He's about to come see you, and it's not gonna be pretty. Can you imagine having God clearly laying out what He's done to turn you from your sin and then condemning you with the truth that you have failed to listen? The unfortunate truth is that we've all done this, and sometimes we still do. How? By ignoring the Holy Spirit's prompting. Regardless of where you are in your spiritual journey, God is still refining each of us. Are we listening? Are we willingly participating in the process?

In part, Colossians 2:7 tells us that we should,

Let your roots grow down into him and draw up nourishment from him. See that you go on growing in the Lord, and become strong and vigorous in the truth you were taught (TLB).

God is asking us to sink our roots into who He is, into His Word, and to draw up the life He offers. We need to become firmly anchored so that no matter what storms come, we cannot be moved because He is the core of who we are. As we do this, He will break apart the things in our life that we've created and replace them with what He has for us.

Have you ever seen an abandoned house that's been taken over by nature? It's always surprising and sad to see trees growing inside the walls of what used to be a home. Tree roots are extremely powerful and destructive. The whole purpose of the root structure is to anchor the tree and to provide nourishment. The root starts out very thin and almost looks fragile. But that thin root will lodge itself in a crack and grow. As it grows, the root will expand the crack that allows water in, which widens the crack, allows the root to grow, and allows more water in, which... The end result is the destruction of the walls, roofing, masonry, etc. until there's very little evidence that a house ever existed there. This gradual process began with the home not being properly attended to and eventually abandoned.

It's the same way with any sin or disobedience that's in our lives. If we don't attend to it right away, we're allowing our relationship with Christ to deteriorate. Over time, that area gets weaker, more compromised, and begins to rot. The length of time this takes in our lives may vary, but the outcome is the same. If we neglect the leading of the Holy Spirit, if we turn a deaf ear to God's voice, then we're putting into motion our own destruction.

Discussion Questions

1. What do you think about God telling Israel that ignoring His warnings will never be forgiven?

2. Could that apply to us today? How?

3. What are you doing to become more firmly anchored in who God is?

❖49❖

What Did You Come to Give?

God tells the Israelites that when their 70-year exile in Babylon is over, He'll bring them back to the Promised Land, saying,

"For I know the plans I have for you," declares the Lord, "plans to prosper you and not to harm you, plans to give you hope and a future. Then you will call on me and come and pray to me, and I will listen to you. You will seek me and find me when you seek me with all your heart. I will be found by you," declares the Lord, "and will bring you back from captivity" (Jeremiah 29:11-14, NIV).

Jesus illustrates the kingdom of heaven saying,

Suppose one of you has a hundred sheep and loses one of them. Doesn't he leave the ninety-nine in the open country and go after the lost sheep until he finds it? And when he finds it, he joyfully puts it on his shoulders and goes home. Then he calls his friends and neighbors together and says, "Rejoice with me; I have found my lost sheep" (Luke 15:4-6, NIV).

Jesus says, *"When I am lifted up from the earth, then all of humanity will be drawn to Me"* (John 12:32, VOICE).

God tells us, *"I will be your God through all your lifetime, yes, even when your hair is white with age. I made you and I will care for you. I will carry you along and be your Savior"* (Isaiah 46:4, TLB).

Those are tremendous promises made by the Creator of the universe! If we're seeking after God, we will find Him. If we're lost,

He will come looking for us. Jesus draws us to Himself so we can experience the love, forgiveness, restoration, and transformation He offers. In return, we're to follow Jesus' instructions in Matthew 16:24: Cease to be who we were, stop doing the things we used to do, put our sinful nature to death at every opportunity, and follow Him forever.

> Paul said, *"For we are to God the pleasing aroma of Christ among those who are being saved and those who are perishing"* (2 Corinthians 2:15, NIV).

> Jesus told us, *"Let me tell you why you are here. You're here to be salt-seasoning that brings out the God-flavors of this earth. If you lose your saltiness, how will people taste godliness? You've lost your usefulness and will end up in the garbage"* (Matthew 5:13, MSG).

In her on-line daily devotional, Christine Caine points out,

There's a direct correlation between us relishing the God-journey we're on and the aftertaste we leave in our relationships with others. What taste is left in people's "mouths" after an encounter with you? Did they taste the goodness of God through your words and actions, or were they left with a bitter aftertaste?[1]

There was a little Italian restaurant that my wife and I really liked. It took a while for the food to come out, but it was worth the wait because everything was so good! You could taste the wine, the parmesan cheese, the basil, and the garlic in the sauce, and we'd eat every molecule. The problem was that we could still taste it the next afternoon. As good as their food was, we eventually quit going because we didn't like that aftertaste.

I have to wonder if that's true for me. Do people at work see the old me or do they see Jesus' work in me? I'm not interested in being "all things to all people" or even overly concerned with pleasing people, but do my actions and my interactions with people reflect who He is? No matter the circumstances, I want to make sure that I leave His imprint on someone's heart after we've parted ways.

A life group my wife and I were part of would go on a weekend retreat every couple of years. One year we gathered together on a Saturday afternoon, and one of the ladies had a word from God. In it He asked us, "Why are you here? What did you come to give?" That hit me hard! I hadn't come to "give" anything—I'd come to *get*! That's an easy mindset to fall into, but in order to be refined and purified, we have to willingly give ourselves over to that process. We have to deliberately go before God and ask Him to show us what doesn't belong in our heart or our life.

Over and over again in the Bible, God tells us that He wants *all* of us. He's up front about that and even warns us that He's a jealous God that won't share any of our affection or allegiance with anything. However, this isn't a one-way street. In return for all of us, He gives us all of Himself. God needs *nothing*, but He wants our heart.

Discussion Questions

1. What does it mean to you to understand that you were the "one lost sheep" that Jesus came to find and save?

2. Does your life reflect Jesus in a way that would please His heart?

3. We say that we've come together to seek His face and draw closer to Him. But what did you come here to give?

1 Christine Caine, *First Things First with Christine*, 8/25/2016

✤50✤

Ownership of Our Spiritual Relationship

For the past week I've been stuck on the thought, *Do we own our relationship with Jesus Christ, or are we mostly just doing what we should?* So, I'd like to look at three relationships: one where the person was positioned by God and failed miserably; one that was deeply involved but not fully committed at the heart level; and one that was fully committed to accomplishing all that they were given to do and ensuring God's laws were followed.

First Kings 11-13 details the breakup of the nation of Israel, which went from twelve unified tribes to the tribe of Judah and everyone else. The cause was Solomon's sin and the failure of his son, Rehoboam, to listen to wise counsel. God sent a prophet to Jeroboam, who was overseeing a construction project for Solomon. He let him know that ten tribes would be taken away from Solomon and given to him to rule. God made sure Jeroboam knew that reason for dissolution of the nation was due to Solomon's idol worship.

But I will take away the kingdom from his son and give ten of the tribes to you. His son shall have the other one so that the descendants of David will continue to reign in Jerusalem, the city I have chosen to be the place for my name to be enshrined. And I will place you on the throne of Israel and give you absolute power. If you listen to what I tell you and walk in my path and do whatever I consider right, obeying my commandments as my servant David did, then I will bless you; and your descendants shall rule Israel forever (1 Kings 11:35-38, TLB).

Everything happens as God said it would. Once Jeroboam is made king over the ten tribes that revolted, he has an epiphany.

Unless I'm careful, the people will want a descendant of David as their king. When they go to Jerusalem to offer sacrifices at the Temple, they will become friendly with King Rehoboam; then they will kill me and ask him to be their king instead. So on the advice of his counselors, the king had two golden calf idols made and told the people, "It's too much trouble to go to Jerusalem to worship; from now on these will be your gods—they rescued you from your captivity in Egypt!" (1 Kings 12:26-28, TLB)

God made Jeroboam the same promise that He'd made to David and established Jeroboam's kingdom. Instead of trusting God to secure his rule, Jeroboam instituted idol worship—the exact reason God tore ten tribes away from Solomon. Jeroboam was positioned by God, had His promise in hand, yet chose to worship idols as a means of holding onto that promise.

In Matthew 10:1-40 Jesus sent His disciples out to preach that the kingdom of heaven has come, to heal the sick, raise the dead, and drive out demons. Judas Iscariot was one of the disciples that went out preaching, healing, and directly experiencing God's power flow through them. Judas walked all over Israel with Jesus and the other disciples. They didn't catch the subway or hop on a bus—they walked from one place to the next. That's a lot of bonding time. They could only have had superficial discussions for so long, and at some point, things had to get real among everyone.

Judas was *in the boat* when Jesus walked on water. He was there when Jesus fed thousands of people with a few loaves of bread and a couple fish. He was there when Lazarus was raised from the dead. Judas had a front row seat for every miracle Jesus performed. He heard every parable Jesus told and was there when they were explained. When Jesus told the parable of the sower in Luke 8:1-15, I wonder which "soil" Judas identified with? Did he see himself as the good soil, the rocky ground, the thorny area, or the hard path? I'm sure he wanted to be the good soil, but the truth is that Judas was the thorny area.

Judas wasn't on the periphery of Jesus' ministry. He was one of the twelve, the core group that was handpicked by Jesus. He had done life on an intimate level with Jesus and the other disciples. He was right where he should've been and doing many of the things he should've been doing, yet he didn't fully commit his heart to any of it. He didn't have ownership of the relationship.

In chapter 1, Nehemiah received news that the Israelites who had gone back to the Promised Land were faring poorly. The initial group went with Ezra roughly thirteen years prior, and Nehemiah heard that they're still living in disgrace with the walls of Jerusalem torn down and the gates burned. That initial group had rebuilt the temple, but they were still surrounded by broken walls and burned gates—a constant reminder of their punishment and the fact that they were being ruled over by their enemies. He wept and fasted for days in mourning. Then he prayed:

O Lord, God of heaven, the great and awesome God who keeps his covenant of unfailing love with those who love him and obey his commands, listen to my prayer! Look down and see me praying night and day for your people Israel. I confess that we have sinned against you. Yes, even my own family and I have sinned! We have sinned terribly by not obeying the commands, decrees, and regulations that you gave us through your servant Moses. Please remember what you told your servant Moses: "If you are unfaithful to me, I will scatter you among the nations. But if you return to me and obey my commands and live by them, then even if you are exiled to the ends of the earth, I will bring you back to the place I have chosen for my name to be honored. The people you rescued by your great power and strong hand are your servants. O Lord, please hear my prayer! Listen to the prayers of those of us who delight in honoring you. Please grant me success today by making the king favorable to me. Put it into his heart to be kind to me" (Nehemiah 1:5-11, NLT).

God gave Nehemiah favor with the king, and he was permitted to go back to Jerusalem for the purpose of rebuilding the city. Upon his arrival, he immediately set about surveying the damage and formulating a plan on how to accomplish the work. Nehemiah faced significant intimidation from other rulers in the area, had to avoid meetings that were thinly disguised attempts to assassinate him, and dealt with greed and sin reemerging within the Israelite community. Through it all, he stayed focused on pleasing God. He did not waver. He did not falter. Nehemiah was fully committed to rebuilding Jerusalem and to ensuring that the people lived according to the laws that God had given them.

God promises us that,

I will be your God throughout your lifetime—until your hair is white with age. I made you, and I will care for you. I will carry you along and save you (Isaiah 46:4, NLT).

God does everything possible for us to enter into a relationship with Him. He pursues us. He's always there for us and will never leave us. The Bible refers to us, the church—His people—as the Bride of Christ. That's such a powerful image because it references the most intimate relationship we can have with another person. It gives us an indication of the depth and breadth of the relationship we can have with God.

Over and over again, God tells us that He wants an all-consuming relationship with us. He could've made us puppets that dance to His whims, but instead, He gave us the freedom to choose whom we serve so we could pick Him! There is *no* doubt that He loves us and has done everything possible to draw us into a relationship with Himself.

Discussion Questions

1. How do you avoid religion and instead, develop a relationship with God?

2. When it comes to Jesus, do you view yourself as having an active relationship with Him?

3. Are you protecting your heart and mind so that you're not pulled away from Jesus?

✦51✦

The Only Thing

In his book, *From the Pinnacle of the Temple,* Dr. Charles Farrah says,

> The Gospel is understood as that which supplies man's needs, but it is not understood to be that which costs a man everything. We have read His demands so many times that they have lost their potency, but His demands are total (p.93).

The first time I read the words, "We have read his demands so many times that they have lost their potency," I had a bit of righteous indignation and thought, *How can he say that?* But sadly, there is truth to it.

Hebrews 4:12 tells us that,

> *The word of God is full of living power. It is sharper than the sharpest knife, cutting deep into our innermost thoughts and desires. It exposes us for what we really are* (The Book).

In Matthew 18 Jesus tells us that we need to become as little children in order to see the kingdom of heaven. I thought about those passages and Dr. Farrah's comment about God's Word losing its potency. Unfortunately, he's right *if* we allow him to be. We need to pick up the Bible, expecting that it will come alive and that it will apply to us. We have to see it and read it as if for the first time, like a child filled with wonder and excitement.

I remember the first time I took my daughter to see the trains near my parent's house. We waited a little while, and then we saw one coming around the corner way down the line. We could barely see the black outline with its single headlight shining out. As it drew near, we felt the ground rumble, and we were rocked by the wave of air pressure as the train blasted by. The engineer saw us, waved, and blew the horn. It was so loud that she had to cover her ears! She stood there just soaking in the sights, sounds, and power of the train. As soon as it had passed, she ran up and touched the rails just to see what they felt like. *That* is the impact God and His Word should have on us if we're seeking Him.

In 1 Chronicles 21, David buys a threshing floor, oxen, wooden tools, and even the grain in order to build an altar and make atonement for his sins. The guy who owned it offered to give it to David, but his response in verse 24 is,

> *No, I insist on buying it for the full price. I will not take what is yours and give it to the Lord. I will not present burnt offerings that have cost me nothing!* (NLT)

We have to own our walk of faith and it will cost us something. What do I mean by "cost us something"? In my case, I've struggled with anger for most of my life. My refining process has had me in situations where I simply could not react in the ways I always had. My normal thoughts, actions, etc. all had to be abandoned. The costs were to my pride because I felt like I was putting up with garbage that I shouldn't have to and to my sense of control in those situations because the only thing I could control was my obedience to what God was telling me in that moment. It even cost me that part of my identity. I'd been an angry person for so long that I had to figure out who I was without it my life.

Regardless of whether you struggle with anger, substance abuse, purity, pride, or whatever—that area of weakness will be refined through the work of the Holy Spirit, and it will become an area of strength. It's not behavior modification; it's understanding where our redemption and strength comes from, seeing ourselves as God sees us, and then walking it out. We have to own it.

We aren't saved from sin's grasp by knowing the commandments of God because we can't and don't keep them, but God put into effect a different plan to save us. He sent his own Son in a human body like ours—except that ours are sinful—and destroyed sin's control over us by giving himself as a sacrifice for our sins. So now we can obey God's laws if we follow after the Holy Spirit and no longer obey the old evil nature within us (Romans 8:3-4, TLB).

You were dead in sins, and your sinful desires were not yet cut away. Then he gave you a share in the very life of Christ, for he forgave all your sins, and blotted out the charges proved against you, the list of his commandments which you had not obeyed. He took this list of sins and destroyed it by nailing it to Christ's cross (Colossians 2:13-14, TLB).

The thing that caught my attention in both of those passages is the word, "destroyed." God doesn't annotate the Book of Life with, "Forgiven of sins (again) at 0830 on 5 November 2016." No. It says that He *destroyed* sin's control over us and *destroyed* the list of the sins we've committed all because of what Jesus did on the cross. We are free to live for God and free to walk in all He has for us. We are *His* children, and we're told that we can come boldly before Him asking for anything that He said we could have.

So why don't we always pray powerful, purposeful, intense prayers like we do when times are tough? Why do we go from taking an authoritative stance in Jesus' name and fall back to praying weaker prayers? God is the same regardless of our situation, so why do we move to a lesser position simply because we're not in the middle of a trying time? Satan is more aware of the power of prayer than we are because he is subjected to it *every day*. We have to pray like it matters at all times, because it does.

The God who was with David when he wrote in Psalm 22:6 "I am a worm, not a man, scorned and despised by my own people and by all mankind" (TLB) is the same God who was with David when he wrote Psalm 145:1-3, "I will praise you, my God and King, and bless your name each day and forever. Great is Jehovah! Greatly praise him! His greatness is beyond discovery!" (TLB)

We can't live with the focused intensity we have when we're in the "valley of the shadow of death" because we're not always there. But we can, and should, take the lessons learned in the valley and apply them on the mountain top.

A couple things are becoming clearer to me over time. First, the things we hold dear (our possessions, our status) don't really matter in the long run. If you don't believe me, go to an estate sale. You'll find a lifetime of prized possessions on display and on sale. I've gone to quite a few of these, and in many ways, it's a sad experience, but it serves as a great reminder not to get hung up on material things. It's just stuff. Second, when the pressures of life really ramp up, we're suddenly way more able to focus on God, and it's easier to ignore the worldly voices that call out to us. So, I guess that I actually have only one realization: the only thing that is truly important is our relationship with Jesus Christ. Everything else flows from there.

Discussion Questions

1. How can you prevent Dr. Farrah's observation, "We have read his demands so many times that they have lost their potency" from being true for you?

2. If God has destroyed the grasp of sin, death, and the grave on us, why is that we allow ourselves to once again be bound up by them?

3. How can you live and walk in the full power of who God is and what He offers every day?

✦ 52 ✦

Being a Son

I helped my dad do some work on the house I grew up in as it was being prepped for sale. The time we spent together was physically challenging, but I enjoyed being with my dad. As I prepared to leave, I gave him a hug, and he held onto me. I immediately recognized what was happening. That's the same hug I give my kids. It's a precious, lingering moment that conveys more love and emotion than words ever could express. I was seriously choked up. As I reflected on it later, I realized that I had forgotten what it's like to be a son. It also registered in me that this applies to my spiritual life, but I couldn't really articulate how. Here's what I currently understand.

In Genesis 25:27-34, we read about Esau coming back from an unsuccessful hunting trip. When he arrived back at camp, he was starving! Fortunately, his twin brother, Jacob, was there and had a pot of stew going. Esau asked Jacob for a bowl and verses 31-34 recount what happened next.

> *Jacob said, "Sell me your birthright now." Esau said, "I am about to die; of what use is a birthright to me?" Jacob said, "Swear to me now." So he swore to him and sold his birthright to Jacob. Then Jacob gave Esau bread and lentil stew, and he ate and drank and rose and went his way. Thus Esau despised his birthright* (ESV).

Esau likely forgot all about the deal he struck and went on living as he saw fit. When his father was about to die, Esau went hunting in order to prepare his father's favorite meal and then obtain the blessing as first-born. Through an elaborate deception,

Jacob ended up tricking his blind father and obtained the blessing Esau sought. Later, Esau returned with the wild game he had killed. He prepared the special meal his father asked for, brought it to him, and only then learned what his brother had done. He begged for something, anything, from his father and received a blessing that was substantially less than what he gave to Jacob. Esau only cared about his immediate needs and wants; he didn't care about what it meant to be the first-born son. It was only when his father was about to die that Esau sought to take his rightful place. By then, it was too late.

I remember being in kindergarten and having contests with the other boys where we bragged about our dads. Now you have to understand that it wasn't really about the dad. We were declaring our toughness based on how many crackers our dad could eat at one time. "Oh yeah? Well, *my* dad eats this many, all in one bite!" Remember, this was kindergarten, and we were five.

Without getting into the philosophical stuff, the thing that stands out to me now is that I based who I was, and my own sense of strength, on my dad. I remember being so impressed with his ability to fix things. I wanted to be like him so much that I started doing yardwork in order to be big and strong like him. That worked out for one of us better than the other, but the point is that I based who I wanted to be on who my dad was.

One time my dad sent me into an auto parts store to purchase a specific item. I was pretty nervous that I would get the wrong thing or that the guy behind the counter would treat me poorly. My dad gave me all the confidence I needed, telling me, "Just tell him you're my son, and you'll be fine."

Jesus never forgot that He was a Son. In John 5:16-45, He plainly talks about who His Father is, saying,

"My Father is always at his work to this very day, and I too am working" (v. 17 NIV).

"The Son can do nothing by himself; he can do only what he sees his Father doing, because whatever the Father does the Son also does. For the Father loves the Son and shows him all he does. Yes, and he will show him even greater works than these, so that you will be amazed" (v. 19-20 NIV).

"By myself I can do nothing; I judge only as I hear, and my judgment is just, for I seek not to please myself but him who sent me" (v. 30 NIV).

Jesus' identity and strength were given to Him by the Father. Jesus was able to walk the earth in righteousness and holiness because He knew who His Father was and why He was here. I too knew who my father was and what he stood for, yet at some point, I decided to go my own way, pursuing things I knew I shouldn't.

Revelations 12:10 tells us that Satan accuses us of our sins before God day and night, but the accusations don't stop there. Satan loves to remind me of things I've said and done. I can't deny any of what he says; it's all true. It makes me cringe; it makes me feel unworthy; it reminds me of who and what I was. *Was.*

We all have taken steps to become the person we were never intended to be. In doing so, we've given our accuser plenty of ammunition to hurl at us. Like the Prodigal Son, we don't deserve to be a servant in God's Kingdom, much less a son. God knows everything we've said, done, thought—all of it. He was right there when we did it. Yet He has compassion and forgives us. He pulls us close, tells us He loves us, restores us as a son, and celebrates the fact that we're home.

Yes, consequences must be walked out, behaviors and thought processes need to be unlearned, but He's with us through all of that. He doesn't punish us, berate us, or give little digs to make us feel bad on occasion. He simply loves us. He shows us how to move forward—away from the person we became and towards the one we're supposed to be. He speaks truth and life to us, bringing about healing and restoration. Psalm 103:2 says,

> *How far has the LORD taken our sins from us? Farther than the distance from east to west!* (CEV)

If *God* doesn't remember our sins or hold them against us, why should we allow Satan to remind us of them and cause us to limit ourselves? We need to remember that we're sons of the Lord God Almighty and start living like it.

Discussion Questions

1. How does God turn you around and bring you back to Himself?

2. How do you silence Satan's reminders of who you were and focus on the person Christ is changing you into?

3. Do you view yourself as a child of God, having a purpose and position in the kingdom of God?

Final Thoughts

My hope is that as you have read *Locking Shields,* you've been challenged and blessed. Most importantly, I hope you've drawn closer to Christ. If you're considering leading a men's group, this section is intended to provide basic guidance for you.

The first thing to understand is that it will be God's group. You might facilitate the meeting, create the schedule, send the emails, etc., but it is *His* group. The only reason for meeting is the pursuit of a relationship with God and to allow His refining work to draw you closer.

I've seen men's groups take many different forms. Some meet in a church hall with breakfast being served, others meet in a conference room at a local restaurant, and others in an internet-based forum. Most of the groups I've been part of met at 8 am on a Saturday morning. It might seem early, but those that show up want to be there, and that makes a difference. The group I led was, in the words of one associate pastor, "lacking in enticements." We didn't serve breakfast or have coffee or donuts. We were there on purpose and for a purpose. We got in, got after it (dedicating time to pursuing Jesus), and still had a full day to knock out projects around the house or help someone move, etc.

Regardless of where we would meet, the purpose was always clear: to encourage and challenge each other as we pursued Jesus. Because of that, our time together was always powerful. Pray about starting a group, and He will direct you as to the when, how, where, who, and so on.

The bulk of my experience has been with groups that had a dedicated meeting place. Whether in someone's home or a room at the church, we were able to worship openly and speak plainly and in confidence. With that framework in mind, I offer the following:

Always remember that this is *His* group. It is never about you.

It is always about Him, so don't take wrongful ownership of it or allow yourself to become prideful.

The order of events should be simple and consistent. We'd open with prayer, have 10-12 minutes of worship, pray after the last song, go through the lesson (roughly 15 minutes), and enter into the discussion time. As we approached the end of our meeting, the discussion was brought to a close, and we'd literally huddle up to close in prayer. Guys would linger for a bit, but starting and ending on time matters. Everyone is giving up something to be there, and we need to honor their commitment by sticking to the schedule as closely as possible.

Get to your meeting location early and make sure everything is set up. The guys should be able to walk into a space that's arranged and ready to go. If you're playing worship music, have it set up as a separate playlist so you can simply hit "play," and it's rolling. Test the connection to make sure it's up and running. Approach the set up and preparation with the same clarity and purpose as you would an important meeting at work. When the meeting is over, put the place back together as you found it. Don't leave it a mess. Remember, people will be watching to see how you conduct yourselves.

You will have more people who sign up than will show up. So, don't worry about the numbers. Stay focused on what God is doing in your life and in the lives of those who do come.

In order to foster openness and honesty, you will have to set the tone. If you're facilitating the meeting or discussion, you will likely have to go first in opening up about what you're hearing, understanding, going through, struggling with, etc. "Leaders lead" isn't a trite phrase; it's the truth. It's important to understand that leading isn't the same thing as controlling. My absolute favorite group meeting is one where I got exactly one paragraph into the lesson, and a guy said, "Okay, I gotta stop you right there." As the discussion progressed, I was able to sprinkle in all the scriptures

God guided me to as I prepared the lesson. *My* thoughts weren't needed, *His* Word was.

Follow the Holy Spirit's leading. If you follow what God is saying and doing as the meeting progresses, your time together will be meaningful and powerful. The whole point of getting together is to pursue a relationship with Jesus Christ. So, if He is guiding you somewhere—go!

That's it! In closing, I will leave you with a promise from God.

If my people, who are called by my name, will humble them-selves and pray and seek my face and turn from their wicked ways, then I will hear from heaven, and I will forgive their sin and will heal their land (2 Chronicles 7:14, NIV).

About the Author

GEORGE OAKES is passionate about his relationship with Jesus Christ, serving his family, and building genuine personal relationships. He can regularly be found working in the yard, finishing one of many projects around the house, or thinking of ways to convince his wife that owning a '60s era muscle car is a fantastic idea. A retired Marine, George lives with his wife, two children, and one dog in Georgia.

Contact Information
LockingShieldsBook@gmail.com
www.locking-shields.com

CPSIA information can be obtained
at www.ICGtesting.com
Printed in the USA
LVHW081903250721
693406LV00018B/340